Is There A Grandfather In The House?

IS THERE A GRANDFATHER IN THE HOUSE?

A STRAIGHTFORWARD TALK TO CHRISTIAN LEADERS IN TRANSITION

RON A. BISHOP

Is There a Grandfather in the House?

Printed in the USA
Library of Congress Control Number: 2016903123

ISBN (Print): 978-0-9973515-0-7   ISBN (Kindle): 978-0-9973515-1-4

Cover Design: Joseph & Doryann Rohrs
              Graphic Design | Studio City, CA | www.JosephRohrs.com
Front Cover Photograph: Ron Bishop

Prepared for Publication By Palm Tree Productions: www.palmtreeproductions.com
Published by Shepherd Shapers®: www.shepherdshapers.com

To Contact the Author:

WWW.SHEPHERDSHAPERS.COM

DEDICATION

Wayne Beadles is proudly a husband, father, grandfather, and great grandfather. Wayne was born as Marion DeWayne Beadles to his parents Henry and Edith Beadles on 19th September 1921, in Winslow, Indiana.

Wayne's father was a coal miner and farmer. His grandfather, William Green Beadles was born in 1836 and fought on the Union side in the American Civil War.

Wayne Beadles served in WWII in the US Army/Navy as a communications operator and was assigned to the Mediterranean Theater of Operations. This service of duty took Wayne into North Africa, Sicily, Italy and France. He served aboard the USS Biscayne (AVP-11) in the Mediterranean.

During that time Wayne had a spiritual awakening that changed his life.

Wayne, as well as his group of 12 radio operators and 12 cryptographers, received a letter of commendation for a job well done during the Naval Operations overseen by Rear Admiral Richard L. Conolly. Conolly served his country in both WWI & II, and would go on to serve as Full Admiral of the US Navy.[1]

Christi and I have known Wayne Beadles for 40 years, as a man of excellent character and gentleness. He has been a team player with sound wisdom, excellent perspective, a positive worldview, and a manly authority; yet remains a man who doesn't require the outcome to go his way. At age 94, Wayne is still an active Charter Elder at Destiny Church, San Antonio, Texas. His wisdom has been a mainstay, serving the church as a pillar and a backbone, during 69 of the 75 years of the church's history. He has served as assistant pastor, associate pastor, world missions pastor, board member and elder. Married to Inis, the love of his life, for 71 years, they have three sons, seven grandchildren and seven great grandchildren. Their sons are: Ron, Barry and Don.

I asked Wayne for his secret to living a long life? This is what he said: "A happy person lives longer than those who complain. Paul said, though in prison at that time, 'I think myself happy'.[2] Live for the Lord and invest in others. If you bless others, then you will find your life's purpose." Wayne says, "I want to be like Daniel and have an excellent spirit." One of Wayne's favorite scriptures is, "A merry heart doeth good like a medicine: but a broken spirit drieth the bones."[3]

I asked Wayne for his advice to those who want to be a good grandfather? "Be compassionate, understanding and loving. Spend as much time with your descendants as you can. Let them know you appreciate and have confidence in the younger generations. Our example is more than our words; the lives we live speak louder than our words."

I asked Wayne for his advice for those who want to finish strong? He responded, "Keep a positive outlook, pray every morning and night, and don't look at circumstances. I ask God every day to use me. If you look to the Lord for His help; He will help you finish strong."

So, my guess is that Wayne will remain with us for a few more years, and my hope is that he will at least complete 100 years. He has the stamina, the energy, and the drive to make it all the way. We all pray for his health and that, we will be blessed by his presence and his fellowship for more years to come. Wayne, you are now a nonagenarian,[4] but we are hoping you'll make the title of centenarian. We wish you God's very best, Wayne and Inis Beadles.

Endnotes_____

1. www.arlingtoncemetery.net/rlconolly.htm ~ Richard Lansing Conolly, Admiral, United States Navy

2. Acts 26:2 KJV "I think myself happy, king Agrippa, because I shall answer for myself this day before thee touching all the things whereof I am accused of the Jews."

3. Proverbs 17:22 KJV

4. mathforum.org/library/drmath/view/58463.html; sexagenarian = 60s, septuagenarian = 70s, octogenarian = 80s, nonagenarian = 90s, centenarian = 100, supercentenarians = 110 years old and up (No upper limit)

ACKNOWLEDGEMENTS

John Mortimer, Jr.

World Harvest on the Amazon River, Iquitos, Peru

Thank you, John Mortimer, Jr of Iquitos, Peru, for asking me a hard question early that Sunday morning, about how to deal with certain kinds of transitions for leaders. A few hours later, while praying for the right answer, I heard the Lord ask me a question, which became the seed for this book. The words resounded in my head, "Is there a Grandfather in the House?" From that question and my search for the answers, I walked through each of the chapters, which are contained within these pages. I admire the work you and your family are doing to bless the Peruvians. Your team has grown to include four generations of Mortimers right there on the Amazon River.

Matthew Bell
Pastor of Destiny Church, San Antonio, Texas

Thank you Pastor Matt Bell for your morale support as our pastor and for the blessing you and our home church are to us there in San Antonio, Texas. We are grateful for your example, as a young leader, and for the inspiration we receive from you.

Tom Burke
Pastor of Grace Christian Church, Cork, Ireland

Thank you, Pastor Tom Burke of Grace Christian Church, here in Cork, Ireland. We appreciate how you have stood with us as our home church in Ireland. You help make our stay in the Republic of Ireland a pleasure.

Dory and Joe Rohrs
Graphic Design for the Book Cover

Thank you, Dory and Joseph Rohrs, for the graphic design work you do for us in designing the cover of this book. You raise the bar for talents and gifts.

Cameron Bishop
Our Son, For Your Encouragement

Thank you, Cameron, for encouraging me initially to blog my ideas, which resulted in this book, "Is there a Grandfather in the House?"

Thank you, to my wife of 46 years:

Christina Reed Bishop

And the Mother of our two children:

Son: Cameron Bishop

Daughter: Doryann Rohrs

Cameron and his wife, Letha Bishop
&
Dory and her husband, Joseph Rohrs

Our two children have given us six grandchildren:

Cole Marshall Bishop

Lauren Bethany Bishop

Gwynne Elise Rohrs

Trent David Bishop

Cyrus Gray Rohrs

Cora Miette Rohrs

A Word About the Cover

The cover is a photo taken of the author, Ron A. Bishop, standing beside "The Old Sailor"[1] on Pier Road in Kinsale, County Cork, Ireland, just outside of the Trident Hotel. Legend has it that there was an old sailor who, for a lifetime, fished these waters of the Celtic Sea. Although unconfirmed, this familiar local icon was a fitting landmark to remain, even after his passing. Clearly, this grandfather fits in with the seaside.

I chose to put this old sailor on the cover[2] to remind the reader that you will not always be here in the flesh, but you do want your memory to live on by the principles you live by.

RON A. BISHOP

Endnotes

1. The sculptor of "The Old Sailor" is Graham Brett.

1. The cover design was created by Joseph & Doryann Rohrs. Graphic Design, Studio City, CA, www.JosephRohrs.com

INTRODUCTION

In this book, I am speaking to leaders with a willing heart to learn during times of change. Times of change are good times, in that they are growing times. We must step up to the plate[1] to respond positively, and not to react. Responding is the body language of agreement and affirmation, reflecting progress, while reaction is the body language for disagreement, therefore, showing that we cannot accept the inevitable. It is a fact that change is inevitable and unavoidable. Lets be change agents. Three primary things to consider, as you read this book:

- Be willing to accept transitions to enable and empower the next generation of leaders.

- You can continue being a leader and a blessing, even as the years go by.

- Younger leaders must have the wisdom of older men, if they're to remain wise, relevant and cutting edge.

Life is a journey with myriads of obstacles scattered and scheduled all along the way. We'd like to think of life as a joyous, and carefree trek, but that is just not in the offing. Our life journey is more like an obstacle course from the youngest of youth to the oldest of ages. We cannot expect to go unchallenged, nor should we. The tension of challenge creates the environment for growth and change. Choices, choices and more choices will result in decisions, both good and bad. These are the times when wisdom from above is needed, so that your results, your harvest, and your legacy become exemplary and not noxious.[2] It has been said that, God lays out choices for us, and expects us to seek guidance and wisdom so that we do not falter, or misstep. With God's help we can do all things, but on our own, we will struggle to find the way forward.

God does not "bait and switch" by attempting to trick or deceive us. Rather, He woos us to a level of maturity so that we, hopefully, make decisions based on a clear understanding of how to prepare for eternity. Do not draw your wisdom from humanity, but from divinity. Remember, the One who made us, is Omnipresent[3], Omnipotent[4] and Omniscient.[5] He sees the "big picture" and we need His help.

We need tension, pressure, accountability and redefining constantly. When we're young, we need discipline and when we're old, we need tolerance. A word to the youth is sow your seed carefully as one day you'll look back, and seeing the harvest of your life's work; you'll ask yourself questions like, "Did I sow my seed in the right places?" A word to the aged is, what care have you taken to insure that your legacy will not die with you, and how will you pass it on. This generation needs your depth of reasoning and tenderness of heart. They cannot do well, without your reasoning skills, and they will not be sincere without your tenderness of heart.

"There were 200 captains of the sons of Issachar. They knew and understood the times and had much understanding of what Israel should do. And all their brothers obeyed them."[6]

To "know" reflects a built in grasp of divine knowledge, and to "understand" is even a step above and speaks of wisdom. So many know lots of things, but to then understand what to do with that knowledge requires God's help.

We have our entire lives laid out before us. To some of us our lives will continue many years into the future. To others you're standing in the middle of it all with as much of your history behind as before. And then the rest find that most of your life has passed and still there is expectation for a decade more, or less.

We live for "seventy years ... some even live to eighty. But even the best years are filled with pain and trouble; soon they disappear and we fly away."[7]

The challenge most of us struggle with is having the right attitude, perspective, and worldview for tackling our part of the contest before us. As the years pass, we can get a bit sloppy and fail to discern how to respond to the decisions we have made during those times of change.

Ron A. Bishop

Endnotes

1. ***Cambridge Dictionary of American Idioms.*** Copyright © Cambridge University Press 2003. This idiom is based on the baseball meaning of "step up to the plate," or move into position to hit the ball.

2. www.Dictionary.com ~ synonyms of Noxious are: harmful, poisonous, or very unpleasant.

3. www.Dictionary.com ~ Define Omnipresent: "Present everywhere at the same time."

4. www.Dictionary.com ~ Define Omnipotent: "Having unlimited power."

5. www.Dictionary.com ~ Define Omniscient: "Having complete or unlimited knowledge, awareness or understanding. Perceiving all things."

6. I Chronicles 12:32 NLV

7. Psalm 90:10 NLT

ENDORSEMENTS

Ron Bishop is not a writer first. He is a Bible encyclopedia of knowledge and experience. Ron translates his years of travel, teaching, and ministerial experiences into his writings. Ron and Christi have been dear friends of mine for nearly forty years. His most recent book, "Is there a Grandfather in the House?" is a "helps" book for ministers just like me who are facing transition from forty-eight years of pastoring in one church. It is also a must read for pastoral successors and leaders who will take the baton to successfully launch from the shoulders of their predecessors. This book is about finishing the race well and leaving a legacy that will not be forgotten. I highly recommend, "Is there a Grandfather in the house?"

VIRGIL AMUNDSON, PASTOR

Founded Shell Lake Full Gospel Church, in Shell Lake, WI
Served as Senior Pastor for the last 48 years.
Hosts a world class Missions Conference for the last 29 years.
Raises significant financial support to those who work in 37 nations.
Planted two additional churches in northern Wisconsin.
Served for 29 years on the General Board of the Int'l Ministerial Assoc.
www.ShellLakeFullGospel.com

The stakes are high. Our enemy is real. The Church of Jesus Christ will march forward. The question is not "Will Jesus' Church live or die?" We know Jesus is going to build His Church. The question at hand is "Will your church live or die? Will your church outlive you?" As leaders it's our job to steward well what we've been entrusted, and that includes raising up leaders for the next generation. In "Is There A Grandfather In The House?" Ron Bishop tackles this pressing issue of leadership transition within the church in a way that is clear, thoughtful and most of all helpful. I highly recommend you read through it with your leadership team, work through this process together, get a plan in place, and see the baton of the Gospel passed on to the next generation. The stakes are too high to do anything less.

MATTHEW BELL, PASTOR

Lead Pastor of Destiny Church, San Antonio, TX ~ USA
Fourth Generation Pastor of Destiny Church
Matt's great grandfather, Leonard W. Coote, founded the church in 1941
www.DestinyChurchSA.com

The Bishops have been our friends for nearly 40 years. What an inspiration Ron's ministry has been and continues to be. For one man to be so gifted and anointed in so many areas of ministry from being engaged in evangelism, world missions, as a teacher, as a pastor, counselor, and author is unbelievable. "Is there a Grandfather in the House?" should be in every minister's library. Every minister needs to know that stepping down is eminent. Leaders must have solid insight when it comes to raising up those who follow behind. Such books as this one prove to be priceless. I believe this approach is what God had in in mind from the beginning.

KEN BENSON, PASTOR EMERITUS

Pastored Eagle Heights Church in Burnsville, MN for over 40 years.
Retired in June of 2015 and now serves as Pastor Emeritus
Former National Chairman of the International Ministerial Association
Presently living in: Minneapolis, Minnesota ~ USA

Ron Bishop is a seasoned leader who is grappling with an issue that is seldom addressed - The idea of leadership transference with grace, dignity, intention, and wisdom. In his book he deftly challenges the notion of waiting too long to think about what it means to pass the baton of leadership. The God of Abraham is also the God of Isaac and Jacob. He desires compound blessing. This book will be a help and a value to all leaders - young and old alike who desire to see Gods kingdom advanced, and honored over a span of time that exceeds one generation and makes a sustainable impact in whatever the ministry context may be.

TERRY BRISBANE, PASTOR

Lead pastor at Cornerstone Church in San Francisco, CA for 30 years
B.A. in speech communications from San Francisco State University
M.A. in Theology from Fuller Seminary in Pasadena, CA
Doctor of Ministry from The Kings University in Van Nuys, CA
www.Cornerstone-SF.org

Wise is the leader who exercises discernment and insight in the timing of life's transitions. Ron Bishop's encouragement is to gracefully and courageously make the changes that are necessary. "Is There A Grandfather In The House?" encourages the reader to embrace transitions, while gaining wisdom and insight in the process. Redirecting our energies can bring greater joy and fulfillment.

DAVID COOK, PASTOR

Pastor of International Bible Church, San Antonio, TX ~ USA
Former president of International Bible College, San Antonio, TX
President of Rivers of Redemption, a ministry focused on promoting World Missions
www.IBCTX.org

The Lord is always right on time inspiring my good friend, Ron Bishop, to passionately and purposefully share his heart through "Is There a Grandfather in the House?" This book is a breath of fresh air to church leadership worldwide. Early in the book, Ron rang my bell when he asserted that the relay race of generational, leadership succession was never about the runners, but always about the baton. The fullness and power of the gospel of Christ's kingdom must be passed from generation to generation. After pioneering and pastoring a local church for forty years, my wife, Patty, and I, recently installed our son, Danny and his wife, Jill, as new lead pastors. The church has never been healthier. New life is blossoming on every hand. We don't mind one bit that people in the church affectionately refer to us as Poppy and Bama, just like our grandchildren do. We still walk in spiritual authority and rejoice that the baton is in good hands moving from glory to glory.

DAVID S. DILLON, PASTOR EMERITUS

Founding Pastor of the Rock Church in Franklin, VA
The Dillons built strong works through their teams in several nations.
They remain engaged as overseer of mission's initiatives in Bolivia, Uruguay, Ecuador, and Italy
www.RockFranklin.com

At a time when so many baby boomers are retiring from the ministry, the information in this book is invaluable to assist in the transitioning of leadership. I feel that "Is There A Grandfather In The House?" is a must read. It is evident that God has inspired Ron Bishop for this time. I know I will refer to this book in years to come.

DR. MACEL ELY

Founder of Barnabas Ministries International
BMI is a ministry, to encourage pastors and their families during challenging times.
Serves as presbyter, advisor, and overseer for many congregations.
Presently living in: Knoxville, TN ~ USA
www.BMinistries.org

Ron Bishop is man of many talents and gifting. These talents and gifts are very evident in his book, "Is there a Grandfather in the House?" He explores and gives us insight on how to tap into the resources of a largely neglected part of God's army, the retired Generals. This is a very timely subject, and you would do yourself a favor to put this book on your must read list.

GENE E. EVANS, PASTOR EMERITUS

International Director of FGBMFI, Costa Mesa, CA for 8 years.
Served FGFCMI (The Fellowship), Irving, TX since 1980 in various capacities as,
Board Member, Treasurer, VP and finally as President
Founded two churches: Statesboro, GA and Douglasville, GA
Pastored Believers Fellowship, Douglasville church 1990-2012
In 2012 Pastor Evan's son was installed as pastor in
Believers Fellowship Church

As I read the first chapters of "Is There A Grandfather In The House?" I realized my understanding of my role as a father and grandfather was growing with each turn of the page. Ron Bishop goes straight to the heart of our responsibility to prepare the next generation for their destiny. Then, he gently builds optimism as he weaves the time-tested principles of Scripture into each chapter. You will learn how to make a timely transition and why we must make that succession successfully!

DR. RICHARD L. HILTON, PASTOR EMERITUS

Founding pastor of Calvary Church in Johnson City, TN
Assistant Overseer of Calvary Alliance of Churches & Ministries
Serves as a counselor, Leadership consultant and Life Coach
Author of the book: "Generation to Generation"
www.VisitCalvary.com

Ron, we were at the dining room table, in our home in Los Angeles. It's been over thirty years ago since that afternoon. We all shared our dreams for God's Kingdom. As for the Metcalf's, our dream was birthing a church in the LA area. And for the Bishops, it was to reach and teach leaders in the far-flung-frontiers of the world.

I knew then that you would never stop. You would not stop traveling, learning or teaching God's people! We were young at that time; today we are not! We are fully aware that our destiny is that we have, "come to pass." Transition must not be viewed as an event! It is better done through a process.

Thank you a million times for these magnificent nuggets, and illuminating insights on passing the baton. With the help you have shared in this book, we will do this thing successfully. We will pass the baton; we will win this race!

DON METCALF, PASTOR

Founding pastor of Desert Reign Assembly of God, Downey, CA
Author of the book: "So Blessed"
www.DesertReign.org

There is a real need for guidance in the area of transition in church leadership. It is something that will affect the church either in a positive or a negative way. Having recently gone through a transition myself I realize that it must be approached very prayerfully and cautiously. There is a definite need for wise counsel and Ron Bishop has provided that in his book. I highly recommend it to anyone and everyone who is facing a time of transition.

RON NISSEN, PASTOR EMERITUS

Pastor Emeritus of Elim Church, Houston, Texas
Continuing host of Convocations in Houston, Texas & Belize
www.ElimOasis.org

Thank you, Ron, for the reliable teaching ministry you have brought to us over the years. In your book you have dealt with such a vital issue, "handing over the baton and remaining an active ministry in the work of God." You have addressed the issue of "when the baton falls to the ground, because of a death." This is one of the issues we experienced here in Grenoble, France, at our church. Our pastor, Pierre Truschel passed suddenly in September of 2003. We had a strong ministry team, but did not make all the best decisions.

We had to deal with "hot situations" in some of the churches in our network, and felt unprepared for the challenges. The facts were that most of us did not feel ready to take the helm; none of us had selfish ambitions; we had good relationships, but we could have done better had we been equipped ahead of time. We realize that we succeed, as a church, when the people are comfortable with our decisions and feel that they can trust our judgment. Looking back all has gone well, but it was difficult. We now have good men in place.

CHRISTIAN RIVIERE, RETIRED PASTOR

Considered as a Grandfather in the house
Going into "Francophono" nations where we have mission works established
Teaching in Bible Schools in France and in the Francophone nations
Part of an Apostolic Team with Eglise Evangélique de Pentecote
www.LeChandelier.org

Ron and Christi Bishop have been friends of my wife and I for over thirty years. Ron is an excellent teacher and a world traveler. He has the added experience of many years in ministry with the highest integrity, which makes anything he writes something we should read. He has chosen an excellent subject on transition. Transition is one of the difficult challenges every leader must face and Ron shares excellent advice on how to navigate these tricky waters. We desperately need more fathers and grandfathers of the faith to guide a younger generation through our dangerous times.

DALE YERTON, MISSIONARY STATESMAN

President of a mission organization called The Living Faith, Inc.
Presently living in: Hopkinsville, KY ~ USA
To find books Dale has authored go to: www.DaleYerton.com

CONTENTS

Contents

Is There a Grandfather in the House?

FOREWORD

For several years I served as Dr. Edwin Louis Cole's European Director. During those times I sat in multitudes of conferences where statistics were shared from church leaders from dozens of nations. One thing almost all these leaders would refer to, is the absolute ravaging of their societies due to one defining issue; fatherlessness.

Fatherlessness is the blight of this generation, and any honest study shows that this is the foundational reason behind everything from basic poverty, sex trafficking, domestic abuse, rebellion among the youth, unwanted pregnancy, you name it. Where there is no real "father" there is categorically an extremely low level of general personal mental health.

Ron Bishop brings up another issue asking, "where are the grandfathers?" Great question. Bible history uncovers powerful truths about tri-generational importance. It appears that wherever there were three consecutive generations holding on to Godly principles, there was present the strength and provision of a loving God. How powerful is this truth? Amazing.

Current church history reveals sadly a "legitimate" lack of trust between the generations. I say legitimate, because sometimes each of the "three" dimensions of eldership and upcoming eldership among church life can't seem to get on the same page as to lifestyle, relationship, presentation, etc. much less doctrine itself.

As Ron shares, the element of a true "Grandfather" carries much weight, simply because after putting in 50 to 60 years serving the Lord by pastoring and working with people, one hopefully has learned a few things! Some things ONLY come with many years of experience. However communicating these experiences, and the wisdom gained from years of co-laboring with God in leading and serving His people, needs to be offered from the correct perspective.

Ron shares from his many years of experience, the vital need of doing all that you can to earn the respect of the younger generation, yet without compromising the wisdom and revelation that only comes with age. The extreme importance of what it means to "create legacy" comes through in the "passing of the baton" to the next generation, and how this can take place with grace.

Each level, Grandfather, Father, new Father, must respect and acknowledge the other level, for their own generationally learned wisdom and experience, as we're all to learn from one another. No one generation is superior to the other, however times and culture shifts, necessitate the humility to grasp understanding about what each level has learned or is learning.

Humility in Christ has always and ever will be the dividing line between those who will successfully climb God's mountain, whether this is in ministry or general life itself. This book emphasizes the grace and good spirit that is necessary, in order to value different generations, and how to join arms with each for the common goal of Jesus Christ and His church being magnified.

True fathers in the faith are still way too few. True grandfathers in the faith are even more difficult to find. Therefore I challenge you to not only read Ron's book, but also to pray over what he is revealing to the entire body of Christ. We face incredibly dark times ahead according to God's word, and current affairs in the world, and there has never been a greater divine moment, than that which is right now, for true grandfathers and fathers of the faith to be seen. Trust must be restored where walls have broken down between generations. God's word says, "A three-fold cord is not quickly broken!" So study this book, and yield your heart to its truth. Ask yourself the question as well, "Might God want to use me, to be a grandfather or father to those within the circle of my influence?"

Be blessed as you read "Is There A Grandfather in the House?"

ROD ANDERSON
Senior Pastor
Commonwealth Church
London, England, UK

Endnote

1. Ecclesiastes 4:12 KJV

Is There a Grandfather in the House?

PROLOGUE
IS THERE A GRANDFATHER
IN THE HOUSE?

Wisdom ~ Courage ~ Insight

The Church, in its longing for continuing leadership cries out, "Is there a Grandfather in the house?" Just as when someone has collapsed and needs urgent medical attention, the call goes out, "Is there a Doctor in the house?" We have known of generations of fathers who have established churches and trained up leaders who have certainly made a difference. These leaders have built congregations, which have exerted strong influence touching cities, counties, parishes, states, provinces, nations, continents and the world.

Yet, as we continue onward into the 21st century, so many of those grand leaders are at a crossroads. Many of the seasons of their lives have finished and they're in what is often called, "the final chapters." The big question is how do you take a bow and leave the big stage?[1]

It is tough to observe the CEO[2] of something awaken one day to a new life with no assignment, and diminishing accolades. How could he have been better prepared for this moment? How could status change have been less abrupt for this man? Is there a possibility that, if he had adjusted his approach toward that moment he could have stayed in the game, howbeit in a different role?

"Selah. Pause, and calmly think of that."[3]

Endnotes

1. The Big Stage is like the limelight to be high profile with huge public exposure.

2. Chief Executive Officer (Senior Pastor), Set Man, or Leader in Charge.

3. The Amplified Bible adds a defining phrase to this word, "Selah," so that we stop, for a moment, and give serious thought about what has just been said, allowing the gravity of it to sink into our hearts. One example is Psalm 3:4 AMP - "With my voice I cry to the Lord, and He hears and answers me out of His holy hill. Selah [pause, and calmly think of that]!"

Chapter 1

GIVING DOUBLE HONOR WHEN IT IS DUE

RESPECT~AFFIRMATION~HONOR

Give Double Honor

The years have been good to you! You have served God; met the challenges and are thankful for the opportunity to bless others. Not only that, but you have been blessed by others. You have been a good teacher, pastor, and counselor; now you are about to become a grandfather, not only within your family, but also within the church. You have been honored, and have even received double honor[1], just as the scripture instructs us in 1 Timothy 5:17 (KJV), "Let the elders that rule well be counted worthy of double honor, especially they who labor in the word and doctrine."

Your new life chapter, however, will bring significant changes and adjustments. You have had the perks of salary and benefits, front and center accolades and even "double honor." You've had a long run of things, but now the reality is that you are ready for a change. Diminished benefits and accolades will come and you are prepared for more free time. You will find yourself as a member of the congregation and a normal tithe-paying member at that. It must be said that, if you have seen the benefits of and taken the right steps to become a grandfather in your church, then you will have new spheres of influence and responsibility. It does not come automatically, but only if you have repositioned your worldview and paradigms to coincide with whom you are becoming.

The bigger adjustments will be a few days after the pomp and ceremony have passed. You may question things like: "Am I neglecting my call, or am I no longer true to myself?" You may experience these thoughts unless you take time and opportunity to redefine yourself. If you seriously consider redefining yourself, then you'll find it to be of extreme help, as you will continue your adjustments for some time to come. Please allow me to make some observations. Of course there are exception to every rule and people have lived their lives hugely different to others.

Some who read this book will admit that they have never fully lived to their full potential. They had gifts, or talents, which were never fully developed, due to time or financial constraints, pressures or priorities, but certainly due to choices. Some of us may even be like the servants who were given five talents, two talents, or the one talent.[2] Often in the complexity of life, we make choices that either embrace, or alienate options, which, on another day, or under different circumstances could have been viable.

THE IRISHMAN SAID, "IN IRELAND WE DON'T DO FANFARE." HE WAS RIGHT.

Remember this axiom: You are the "beheld,"[3] and when others look at you, they are the "beholder."[4] You'll always be pastor, or colonel, or governor, or

4

president, so these titles may be in order, when addressed by others towards you. The term double honor is valid, and we most certainly acknowledge its value, especially from the vantage point of the beholder.[5] But, when the focus comes to the one being "beheld,"[6] you must, in your heart of hearts, be you with no titles, special robes, or unique considerations. The reason you must think simply is because, "It's not all about you." You are normal, one among many and will be "one of us" when we all gather around the throne, in heaven. Whatever others give you is wonderful, but as the "beheld," when you look into the mirror, you must be you, without fanfare or special acknowledgements. Humility is vital and required for all of us. To be enamored with oneself is a deep character flaw, because it is derived on the back of self-interest. If we fail to be humble, then we will fall short of the mark. One friend of mine, even from the pulpit, referred to himself as "Dr Dave." This was not a slip up, but would occur three or four times in a single sermon. I really found myself feeling a bit uncomfortable, at times. In my opinion, it was less than humble and even a bit narcissistic.[7]

Humanity is weak and the imminence of mortality reveals more about us than we care to admit. Of course there is the athlete and there is the odd one who accomplishes so much and with such fantastic style that we all salute and cast our crowns at their feet, at least for a moment. And yet, bad days, unclimbable mountains and insurmountable circumstances can bring, even the best, to their knees, thus impairing an individual in some ways.

It is only by the grace and favor of God that a man or woman can abound. The will within us can draw us out, or drive us onward to achievements, which few can accomplish without almost super human powers. For these things we must give honor and commendations. It is a fact that there are levels of leadership that can best be described as "captains of hundreds," and captains of thousands."[8] It is a fact that there are accomplished leaders among us. As we stand facing these men we must give honor, where "honor is due."[9]

When you receive certain titles, they often do not fall away, even after our assignments have come to an end. For example, once a general, always a general. An admiral remains an admiral, and is referred to by those who know him as, the admiral. Each of America's former presidents, are still addressed as Mr President. A former pastor is often still, affectionately called, "Pastor."

And so, as one who is often beholding famous and powerful men, I give them honor. But, before you give out lofty titles to men, take a moment to consider that we are all flesh and blood; we succeed, by the grace and help of the Holy Spirit, and must reflect integrity and true character in every stage of life. When honor is due, then give that honor

SOME JUST DON'T FIT WELL IN A PC WORLD.

unashamedly, but if everything about them is "ego driven" take a step back and pray for them, because they just may need your prayers now, more than a fresh puff of wind. One of my favorite all time pastors and prolific writers, was Jamie Buckingham.[10] He was "real," and humble without reserve. He would not have fit so well in this "politically correct"[11] world, because he was painfully honest. He said these words: "There was the fellow who received the annual humble button at the church banquet, and then had it taken away because he wore it. Maybe the best way to wear the bishop's title, or a doctorate, is to let others honor you, but never honor yourself. In other words, take the office, but never yourself seriously."[12]

Endnotes

1. 1 Timothy 5:17-18 TLB "Pastors, who do their work well, should be paid well and should be highly appreciated, especially those who work hard at both preaching and teaching. For the Scriptures say, 'Never tie up the mouth of an ox when it is treading out the grain—let him eat as he goes along!' And in another place, 'Those who work deserve their pay!'"

2. Matthew 25:14-29 The story of the landowner who went on a journey, but first evaluated his servants, giving each talents according to what he suspected to be their ability, or nature. He had suspicions and would now verify what he had thought.

3. Dictionary.com -Beheld (v.) "To observe, look at, see." As the one beheld, you require nothing but for the people to love you. If you receive more, then that is good. You must think in humility. God is, after all, your source.

4. As the Beholder, then you must decide how you will give to the one you are listening to, as your pastor or mentor. You are being tested on how generously you honor the leader in your giving. His needs must be met.

5. As the beholder, you must be generous and give to bless the one who watches over you.

6. As a spiritual leader, you must serve in humility. This church is not a pyramid, with the leader at the top, but actually, an inverted pyramid, with the "servant leader" at the bottom. - smallbusiness.chron.com/importance-inverted-pyramid-organization-34447. html -Traditional management models are hierarchies. Authority and decision-making power are concentrated at the top of an organizational pyramid. Orders are issued and carried out by subordinates. The inverted pyramid in an organization challenges the traditional model. Advocates argue that the 21st century business environment is characterized by rapid change and requires greater flexibility than traditional organizational approaches provide.

7. Dictionary.com -Narcissistic –having an undue fascination with oneself; vain.

8. 2 Kings 11:10 CEV "Jehoiada brought out the swords and shields that had belonged to King David and gave them to the commanders."

9. Romans 13:7 AMP "Render to all men their dues. (Pay) taxes to whom taxes are due, respect to whom respect is due and honor to whom honor is due."

10. jamiebuckinghamministries.com/charisma-magazine-last-word-columns - Jamie Buckingham (1932-1992) jamiebuckinghamministries.com - Every issue of "The Last Word," published 1982-1992

11. www.merriam-webster.com/dictionary-Definition of Politically Correct: conforming to a belief that language and practices, which could offend political sensibilities (as in matters of sex or race) should be eliminated

12. Charisma Magazine's *"The Last Word,"* by Jamie Buckingham. September 1986 issue entitled "Honor to Whom Honor"

Is There a Grandfather in the House?

Chapter 2

It's About The Baton and Not The Runners

Synergy, A Race Run Well, Teamwork

The church has existed for over two thousand years. The history of the church, and the account of those who have been its leaders is one of change, transition, treachery, betrayal and too seldom, redemption. Jesus said, "I will build my church," and that has taken place. The job of Jesus' building his church has certainly involved the strength and energy of men, in the process. The appearance of this can be seen as a sort of relay race, with one generation passing the baton onward to the succeeding generation.

The Age-Old Debate Over Personalities

Jesus said, "Upon this rock I will build my church, and the gates of hell shall not prevail against it."[1] In this verse the "rock" is referring to the revelation of who Jesus really was, the Messiah. It is not referring to Peter, but to the one the question is all about, and that is Jesus.

Some church movements have made Jesus' conversation with Peter, all about a focus on Peter, instead of the revelation, which Peter revealed by giving the correct answer. Jesus asked, "Who do men say that I am?"[2] Peter responded to Jesus' question when he declared, "You are the Messiah, the Son of the living God."[3] To make Peter the central figure of the church is wrong and false.[4] The central figure of the church is Jesus. The point of this conversation was Jesus' effort to reveal his own identity as the Messiah, and never to elevate Peter. Their conversation was a lesson on focus, so that God's people might get the memo on Jesus' identity as the Son of God.[5]

> HELL CAN PUSH, BUT IT CANNOT WIN, IT WON'T PREVAIL.

Early on people were getting confused and focused on the runners, to the detriment of focusing on the baton. This great historical relay race was never about the runners, but always about the baton; Jesus never intended for church history to only be a generation long. It began in Israel and shall extend to all nations and tribes, races and languages; who will be gathered together before the throne and the lamb.[6]

The Older Runner Must Speed Up To Catch His replacement

The new runner sprints ahead of the runner who is on the track.[7] He then reaches back, almost without a second look at the one who is about to finish his part of the race. The one who is about to pick up the baton must run faster than the one he is about to succeed. The runner who is finishing his part of the race, must speed up to catch the new runner who is now ahead on the track. A lot is invested in the fact that the new runner must be prepared to continue the pace of the runner he is about to relieve. He must receive it gracefully and swiftly.

The runner who is giving up the baton also must hand it off gracefully, to prevent the appearance of fumbling. There can be no question of total and complete trust. It must have the smooth appearance of fluid, with no drag or hesitation. The chemistry of this exchange must be a visible picture of total commitment to the process.

The tired runner must hand it off with deliberation so that his successor feels confident, assured and empowered.[8] The smoothness of "exchanges (of the baton) during the… race are just as important as the speed of the runners. It is a fact that races can literally be won or lost, and all because of a slow or sloppy exchange."[9] It must be clear that this is not about personalities, but about the goal, the assignment and the success of the whole race.

We run as succeeding members of the eternal team, spanning all the way from the days of the early church to the present. We have an apostolic succession, in spite of human failures along the way. This church and all who make up the "Jesus Team" are moving together, in the spirit of Christ, to pass the tools of the trade onward to those who shall follow through to the finish line, when the trumpet shall sound[10] and time shall be no more. Everything depends on the moment of the passing of the baton, so that, when the race is finished, the baton has been carried to its rightful place. The Olympian at the end, seems to get all the honor, but the fact is, all competed in the race,[11] and were carried on the shoulders of that great "cloud of witnesses"[12] to celebrate, at the marriage supper of the lamb.[13]

And the Debate over Personalities Continues

The debate over personalities continued, with the mother of James and John[14] coming on a quest to Jesus to make a request. Her wish was for Jesus to empower her sons by inviting them to become prominent in his Kingdom, allowing them to sit, on his right hand, and on his left.[15] It is amazing how "flesh" is determined to make advances and become prominent even in the realm of the Kingdom of God. They are always aiming for position and often claiming, "It's all about me."[16] Not only in Israel of 2000 years ago, but with those who wish to establish movements since those days.

FLESH ALWAYS
CRIES OUT FOR
ATTENTION.
IT WANTS TO
BE BOSS.

Men just love to puff themselves up and attempt to usurp position. It is a good idea to avoid too much emphasis on titles and self-promotion, whenever possible. There is a dearth of humility, while self-aggrandizement is all the rage.

The reason I have gone down this path in dealing with transition is because of what I have learned about relay races and the passing of the baton. Here is a principle, which must be acknowledged by those who are coming to the place in their lives, when they must pass or receive a baton. "The race is about the baton, not the runners."[17] It is so easy to get caught up with the euphoria of superstars and athletes, but we must not loose sight of what the Holy Spirit wishes to accomplish in the bigger picture. "The objective is to keep the baton moving at maximum speed at all times throughout the race. The baton must always remain the fastest member of the squad!"[18]

Learning to give honor is a valuable part of the character we must exude as we ascribe to being a part of the church. We do want to give honor to our elders, and to those who are in authority over us.

We also want to have a respectful place in our hearts for those who have invested in our lives. This is not a debt, but what we gladly give to each other, from hearts of love.[19]

The subject here is both "the beholder" and the one being "beheld." When it comes to the one looking into the mirror (the one being beheld) we must take a look at ourselves from a different vantage point. We must not be self-focused and require honor, but must walk in humility.[20] The primary reason we need humility, is because we are clay and He is the potter.[21] We must give up our expectations and require no earthly reward, but focus on laying up our treasures in heaven. Of course, we reap what we sow. If we sow respect and honor, then it comes to us from many varied sources and often during our lifetimes.

> "IT WAS PRIDE THAT CHANGED ANGELS INTO DEVILS: IT WAS HUMILITY THAT MAKES MEN AS ANGELS."
>
> -SAINT AUGUSTINE

The Race Is About The Baton, Not The Runners[22]

When sitting in the stands, and watching the runners in the race, we acknowledge the athletes, and cheer them on, but we find ourselves keeping an eye on the baton, because at the end of the day, we are cheering the baton onward. We smile when it is successfully passed on from runner to runner, and are horrified when it is dropped to the pavement.

The value of the runner is, without dispute, a tremendous asset to the Kingdom of God. When a pastor, or a leader successfully passes the baton and his replacement securely grasps it and goes on to finish the race, all creation gets excited.[23] We love to see things done right. We have compassion when there is failure, but, in our heart of hearts, we really do appreciate it when care is taken to do things correctly.

We certainly want to give accolades when a senior man comes to the day when transition to a younger man is to take place. It is a pleasure to watch the transfer of the mantle from one happy grandfather to his son in the Gospel, who has been trained and is primed and ready to go. To accept graciously the role of "decrease" is commendable, especially while standing in the spotlight of the one who now is front and center with all lights on him. One of the challenges facing leaders, who have been prominent for many years, is when they feel the timing of the transfer, or transition, or passing of the baton is fully in their control. Their fear is that they will not be in control of the timing of the transfer. They sometimes are in a measure of denial, either to their own mortality or perhaps the patience or expectations of the incoming leader, or even the church itself. Timetables are often imposed, which extend as much as five years, even though the senior leader is in decline. So much is put at risk, and, too often, largely because of a deep hesitation to pass the baton. In some cases the circle of perspective is getting smaller, just at the time when it should be getting bigger.

WE ARE THE HANDS AND FEET OF JESUS, IN THE EARTH.

Of Course Care Must Be Taken For The Finances Of The Church, But The Baton Will Not Wait For Us

The church is a significant financial institution and care must be taken to insure its stability, assets, and continuance. This is where a team of leaders is desirable and a blessing. Another consideration is that a church, or ministry is unique, in that the "set man"[24] or senior pastor has built a following of loyal supporters. There is often a thought, which is rumored, that his departure could make or break the unity and stability of the institution. This is why it is imperative that he chooses a "Timothy"[25], or "Joshua"[26] as early as possible, and then mentors him into the responsibilities he is expected to assume. If this senior leader has waited until he is near his own "retirement age"[27] then it could jeopardize the process. Planning ahead is imperative when it comes to meeting the challenges of these times. Consider that the relay race began before you were born and is already in process, so let us not impede the building of the church and its progression of movement to reach the next generation, because we struggle with timing. Do practice sessions in your mind, and then it will transition into a dream. When it becomes a dream then you will easily embrace it as what you are really committed to do. This will minimize the struggle, and make it a rewarding exchange.

> INTEGRITY IS THE INTEGRATION OF CHARACTER IN YOU.

God will judge each leader on integrity and sincerity of heart. Integrity is the integration of character into the fabric of an individual. It is vital to have a moral compass that does not waiver, especially when the winds of change and adversity are blowing.

Endnotes

1. Matthew 16:18 KJV

2. Matthew 16:13

3. Matthew 16:16 NLT

4. 2 Peter 1:20 No private interpretations is allowed. It must be consistent with the bigger picture.

5. John 1 - Read the first chapter of the Gospel of St. John in its entirety to see Jesus as the Word, and central to the church

6. Revelation 7:9

7. trackandfield.about.com/od/trackandfieldbasics - I am using as my standard the "4x100 meters Relay Race." And the ground rules given in ***Track and Field Magazine***

8. trackandfield.about.com/od/trackandfieldbasics -"The baton is passed blindly with runners maintaining as much speed as possible during each exchange. The first runner begins in starting blocks, carrying the baton. The second runner stands within a 10-meter acceleration zone that precedes the passing area. As the first runner approaches, the second begins running, enters the passing zone, and then reaches one hand back while keeping his focus ahead. The first runner slaps the baton into the second runner's outstretched hand."

9. trackandfield.about.com/od/trackandfieldbasics - I am using as the standard the "4x100 meters Relay Race." And the ground rules given in ***Track and Field Magazine***

10. Matthew 24:31 KJV "And he shall send his angels with a great sound of a trumpet, and they shall gather together his elect from the four winds, from one end of heaven to the other."

11. Hebrews 11:13 NKJV "These all died in faith, not having received the promises, but having seen them afar off were assured of them, embraced them and confessed that they were strangers and pilgrims on the earth."

12. Hebrews 12:1-3 MSG "Do you see what this means—all these pioneers who blazed the way, all these veterans cheering us on? It means we'd better get on with it. Strip down, start running—and never quit! No extra spiritual fat, no parasitic sins. Keep your eyes on Jesus, who both began and finished this race we're in. Study how he did it. Because he never lost sight of where he was headed—that exhilarating finish in and with God—he could put up with anything along the way: Cross, shame, whatever. And now he's there, in the place of honor, right alongside God. When you find yourselves flagging in your faith, go over that story again, item by item, that long litany of hostility he plowed through. That will shoot adrenaline into your souls!"

13. Revelation 19:6-9 CEV "Then I heard what seemed to be a large crowd that sounded like a roaring flood and loud thunder all mixed together. They were saying, 'Praise the Lord! Our Lord God All-Powerful now rules as king. So we will be glad and happy and give him praise. The wedding day of the Lamb is here, and his bride is ready. She will be given a wedding dress made of pure and shining linen. This linen stands for the good things God's people have done.' Then the angel told me, 'Put this in writing. God will bless everyone who is invited to the wedding feast of the Lamb.' The angel also said, "These things that God has said are true."

14. Mark 3:17 ~ The two sons of Zebedee were James and John.

15. The complete conversation is found in Matthew 20:20-23

16. "It's all about me," is an egocentric song of this generation, sung by both Bratz and Chelsea Staub. Too many subscribe to this mantra or philosophy of life.

17. In an exchange with Dr Jeff Myers, on the subject of: "Mentoring and Passing the Baton." Coach Nigel Hetherington, the Scottish National Sprints and Hurdles coach, shares ten principles of the baton relay. www.allaboutgod.com/mentoring-and-passing-the-baton-faq.htm

18. Coach Nigel Hetherington, the Scottish National Sprints and Hurdles coach.

19. Romans 13:8 NIV "Let no debt remain outstanding, except the continuing debt to love one another, for whoever loves others has fulfilled the law."

20. Proverbs 18:12 GNT In the Living Bible TLB it says it this way, "Pride ends in destruction; humility ends in honor."

21. Jeremiah 18:1-5 NLT "As the clay is in the potter's hand, so are you in my hand."

22. Coach Nigel Hetherington, the Scottish National Sprints, and Hurdles coach.

23. Romans 8:18-19 NLT "Yet what we suffer now is nothing compared to the glory he will reveal to us later. For all creation is waiting eagerly for that future day when God will reveal who his children really are."

24. Numbers 27:16-17 NKJV "Let the Lord... set a man over the congregation... who may lead them out and bring them in, that the congregation of the Lord may not be like sheep, which have no shepherd."

25. Paul chose Timothy, his son in the Gospel, as his successor. 2 Timothy 1:1-2

26. Moses chose Joshua as his assistant and then he became Moses' successor. Joshua 1:1-18

27. Retirement age is that phantom age, when public expectation says that you are to cease from work and step into the less busy lifestyle. The idea, in the United States, is that you should have built a nest-egg of savings, which, when added to the Social Security Administration benefits, should carry you all the way to the end of life. The standard is set in the minds of people, by the age recommended by Social Security benefits, that generally being about 65, or at least between the ages of 60-70.

Is There a Grandfather in the House?

Chapter 3

A Lesson in Point
Henry Higgins, Colonel Pickering & Eliza Doolittle

Just so you'll know the difference for when the focus is on the wrong one, consider watching the movie, "My Fair Lady,"[1] and then you'll recall this situation, which came about. It just does not feel right when the focus is on the wrong party.

This chapter may seem out of line with the nature of the book, as a movie review, but just consider the result of having focused on the wrong ones. It can be devastating and undo the very goal of what things should really be about.

The Storyline

The setting is in London. The film depicts a poor Cockney flower seller, often called a guttersnipe, who overhears an arrogant phonetics professor, Henry Higgins, as he casually wagers that he could teach her to speak "proper" English, thereby making her presentable in the high society of Edwardian London. His subject turns out to be the lovely Eliza Doolittle (Audrey Hepburn), who agrees to speech lessons to improve her job prospects.[2]

The attention, in the movie My Fair Lady, should have been on Eliza Doolittle, but in the end, was totally about the two men, who had made a bet, using the flower girl, as their pawn. The fact was that Professor Higgins had successfully trained the guttersnipe[3] to speak proper English. The bet was that Professor Higgins could pass her off, in English society circles, as a social aristocrat. They would use a formal gathering of such types to put her on display. The whole event was most entertaining. Higgins did succeed in transforming Doolittle's awful street language. He also dressed her up in exquisite finery so that she appeared to be quite a sophisticated lady, who was actually accused of being a princess from Hungary.

She had overwhelmingly passed the test, but it was largely because of her own tenacity, hard work and all on very little sleep. After the final event he and Colonial Pickering should have lavished praise on her for how well she had done. But, no, they never complimented her once, but carried on dancing and singing about how well they had done. The words went on forever, with them dancing, slapping each other on the shoulders and exclaiming: "By George, I really did it, I did it, I did it. I said I'd make a woman and indeed, I did. I knew that I could do it, I knew it, I knew it! I said I'd make a woman and succeed, I did!" Of course, Eliza Doolittle stands in the shadows upset and with the look of disenfranchisement. She should have been the champion, to receive accolades and compliments for a job well done, as the student, but the teacher, Professor Higgens, took all the glory.

Endnotes_____

1. Consider seeing the movie: My Fair Lady (Audrey Hepburn) as Eliza Doolittle; (Wilfrid Hyde-White) as Colonial Pickering and (Rex Harrison) as Professor Henry Higgins.

2. en.wikipedia.org/wiki/My_Fair_Lady_(film) - My Fair Lady is a 1964 American musical film, starring Audrey Hepburn and Rex Harrison.

3. www.thefreedictionary.com/guttersnipe - A street urchin. A person regarded as having the behavior, morals, etc. of one brought up in squalor.

Is There a Grandfather in the House?

Chapter 4

THIS GENERATION NEEDS SPIRITUAL FATHERS

Keep your personal options open. You are faced head on with two generations: Firstly, you are a part of the generation to which you were born. Secondly, you are an authority figure, or father to the younger generation, which is becoming more prominent, by the day.

What Can You Do For Those Who Are Living Today?

How will you give input to those around you? Some of your peers are still with you and you should enjoy them as much as possible. Hopefully, you will enjoy their fellowship or other forms of entertainment with them. But keep in mind that they have charted their own courses in life and are coming to the closing chapters themselves. The younger generation, however, has more energy, more life ahead of them, and, if they see you as being interested in them and willing to make investments in them without strings being attached, you may find willing associations and ready learners.

We were living in the Black Forest of Germany. Our son, Cameron, had left us behind as he pursued his University education. In our home, we were a family of three, with our teenage daughter, Doryann. Every night I would have prayer with her before she went off to sleep. Occasionally, I would make a little speech to her, telling her that, "When you grow up, you must tell your children and grandchildren about me. If you tell them, then you will be, carrying me, with you into the future. However, if you fail to speak of me, then my history and my impact here on earth will cease." She would then assure me, with a big smile, that she would carry me to her family, so that I would continue to live in their hearts. I would then give her a big hug and thank her.

> TAKE ME WITH YOU INTO THE FUTURE SO I'LL NOT BE FORGOTTEN. IF YOU FORGET ME...THEN I'LL CEASE TO EXIST IN THIS WORLD.

When you are no longer the senior leader, but the grandfather, you can walk down paths that involve teaching, fatherly counsel, writing and mentoring, only if you reflect the nature of a loving and caring grandfather. Every young man needs a "father," even those who have grown up and are middle age. I have had younger men (and not even that much younger) ask if I would mentor them. What was it that drew them to me? What was their need that caused them to reflect on their own need to have a spiritual father? A mentor is much like a spiritual father. Sometimes it is because they have a "father wound"[1] and need an older "father type" to affirm and tell them they are okay.

Not every dad is a father. Not every grandfather can speak into a life and exude peace. It is necessary to undergo personal introspection if you have the hope of speaking into the lives of younger men. To have a spirit of peace and to be a contented man is vital if you are to help others. You can only draw from what you have in your own basket. If you do not have peace on the inside, if you have anger issues, if you are offended by anyone, then you will only be able to draw from those sources and give those issues away. You must deal with such things, so that you are healed yourself, before you can heal someone else. Just remember two things: you can only "reproduce after your kind," and whatever is cooking in the kitchen will send the odor all through the house, so, I ask: "What is cooking inside of you?"

> NOT EVERY GRANDFATHER CAN SPEAK INTO A LIFE AND EXUDE PEACE. YOU MUST HAVE THE GLORY OF GOD IN YOUR BASKET.

Don't Accept The Challenge To A Duel[2]

We have all, at some point in our lives, and for any variety of reasons, been challenged to meet an opponent in the street. It is not possible to imagine any man who has never gotten crossways with another man; if not in adulthood, certainly as a kid growing up. At some point in time, someone has thrown down the gauntlet[3] and challenged you to select your weapon of choice. The question is not only, "Who won?" But did you lay aside a peaceful nature and go for a shootout[4] at high noon?[5]

When someone wants to pick a fight with you, take your cue from Dr Billy Graham. I remember watching an interview on the Phil Donahue Show,[6] probably in the early '80s where Donahue, asked Dr Billy Graham his view of the controversial Equal Rights Amendment. The conversation went something like this: "Dr Graham, again I ask you to please tell us what are your views of the Equal Rights Amendment."[7] Graham answered, "I told you earlier that this is not the agreed subject for this interview." "Dr Graham, even Jesus spoke about controversial subjects." Dr Graham answered, with a twinkle in his eye, "Yes, and they crucified him. I don't plan to be crucified today." Donahue was aghast and promptly moved the interview to another subject, so was unable to draw "America's pastor"[8] into a debate that day.

> TAKE YOUR CUE FROM BILLY. I WILL NOT FIGHT TODAY. THIS IS NOT MY BATTLEGROUND.

Some men think, if someone throws down the gauntlet[9] to challenge you, then you must, take up the gauntlet[10] and respond. This is flawed thinking and not really very mature. Just because someone calls you "Chicken," doesn't mean you have to defend your honor. Turn your back on them and walk away. It takes more courage to walk away from most confrontations than to take up the challenge. Whenever possible defend your honor by the example of standing strong and keeping your wits. Yes, there are some battles you must engage in, but generally that is not the case. Walk away and prove you're a better man than the aggressor. If you can be a positive example by not striking back, then you may live to influence another generation of leaders. Take a page out of Dr Billy Graham's playbook and do not do battle, without good cause.

This generation needs spiritual fathers. Where are they going to get them? They should not have to import them, but should be able to find them in their community and you just may be the man.

What Is The Difference Between Coaching & Mentoring?

Two different options can be considered when it comes to giving input into the lives of those who are hungry to get the best results out of their career, ministry, and life in general. You can seek out training to become a "Life Coach," or you can use your life experiences to respond as a mentor. Rather than my attempting to give you an exhaustive study in the differences, it is best you do your own research. There are good places to begin your pursuit.[11]

To serve as a Life Coach you should begin, realizing that it is short term: "A coach can successfully be involved with a coachee for a short period of time, maybe even just a few sessions. The coaching lasts for as long as is needed, depending on the purpose of the coaching relationship."

To serve as a mentor, realize that it is always long term: "Mentoring, to be successful, requires time in which both partners can learn about one another and build a climate of trust that creates an environment in which the mentoree can feel secure in sharing the real issues that impact his or her success. Successful mentoring relationships last nine months to a year."[12]

Endnotes

1. www.actsweb.org *"Healing a Man's Father Wound"* by: Richard Innes

2. Dictionary.reference.com/browse/duel - "Duel" - a prearranged combat between two persons, fought with deadly weapons according to an accepted code of procedure, especially to settle a private quarrel.

3. En.wikipedia.org/wiki/Gauntlet_(glove) - Gauntlet is a name for several different styles of glove, particularly those with an extended cuff covering part of the forearm. Gauntlets exist in many forms, ranging from flexible fabric and leather gloves, to mail and fully articulated plate armor.

4. tvtropes.org/pmwiki/pmwiki.php/Main/ShowdownAtHighNoon - Scenario common in the American West: The disagreement started over whatever offence was committed. One character is required to say, "This town ain't big enough for the two of us." The two men stand at opposite ends of the street, hands hovering over their holsters… Long seconds pass. On a cue known only to the gunfighters, hands slap leather and shots ring out.

5. tvtropes.org/pmwiki/pmwiki.php/Main/ShowdownAtHighNoon - Scenario common in Early modern Europe: The disagreement started after whatever the offence was committed. One character is required to say, "This town ain't big enough for the two of us." Then two men stand back to back in the street. They step forward ten paces, the spurs on their heels clinking with every step. At the tenth step, they turn. The shoot out begins.

6. en.wikipedia.org/wiki/The_Phil_Donahue_Show - The Phil Donahue Show, also known as Donahue, was an American television talk show, hosted by Phil Donahue. It ran for 26 years on national television… broadcast nationwide between 1970 and 1996.

7. www.equalrightsamendment.org/misc/faq.pdf - The Equal Rights Amendment: Frequently asked Questions, July 2015

8. *America's Pastor: Billy Graham and the Shaping of a Nation* – November 7, 2014 by Grant Wacker. "America's Pastor reveals how this Southern fundamentalist grew, fitfully, into a capacious figure at the center of spiritual life for millions of Christians around the world." Some even call Graham, "a plainspoken preacher and the 'Protestant pope.'"

9. Dictionary.com - Throw down the gauntlet - Declare or issue a challenge. This expression alludes to the medieval practice of a knight *throwing down* his *gauntlet*, or metal glove, as a challenge to combat.

10. www.thefreedictionary.com/take+up+the+gauntlet - take up the gauntlet to accept a challenge.

11. www.management-mentors.com/resources/coaching-mentoring-differences - This article deals with the differences between being a "Life Coach" and a mentor. Generally, in the context of church and leadership, a life coach deals with professionalism, leadership guidelines and choices in your life. It may also carry over into secular pursuits and career decisions; whereas, a mentor deals with general questions about life, ministry, family and issues of the heart.

12. www.management-mentors.com/resources/coaching-mentoring-differences-

Is There a Grandfather in the House?

Chapter 5

DO YOU KNOW HIS "HEART OF HEARTS?"

HE MUST HAVE YOUR HEART, OR HE WILL BREAK YOUR HEART!

A WAKE UP CALL

Choosing your Joshua or Timothy may be the Hardest Thing You have Ever Done

When you are choosing a successor, you must not ignore the still small voice of the Holy Spirit, take short cuts, or fail to be true to your better judgment. Just because the one you have in mind to step up to take your job, looks like a "Star," a "Stallion," or a "Super hero," doesn't mean that he will last for the long race of time, or carry the vision of the house to the finish line. Too often those "star studded" heroes prove unable to keep the smile, and do the right thing.

There are few things, in leadership circles, which can cause a grandfather to experience a broken heart more quickly than the sort of betrayal, which can come after a transition takes place. On the day of installation, a young man makes commitments, which he is expected to fulfil, all the way to the finish line. After the transition is complete it is not possible to gather up all the feathers,[1] which have been released. The wind will take those feathers to the ends of the earth. This is why much prayer, and layers of wisdom must be sought after, before the fact. Do not think you are exempt from failure. Without grace, wisdom and most of the gifts of the spirit, working in your life, you could easily set into motion a "train wreck."[2] It is therefore incumbent upon us to look deeply into the mirror to search for humility, and the ability to receive counsel from wiser men, before making these decisions. The challenge before you is to know the difference between a "good idea" and a "God idea." Keep in mind that it is possible to sabotage your own "transitional success" by being so self-absorbed with the euphoria of the transition that you couldn't tell the difference.

It is one thing to choose a David, which bears resemblance to your image, and quite another to select a Saul you have chosen from among the crowd just because of his height, his reputation or the aura he carries. The reality is that in the Bible story of Israel's King Saul, he did have a change of heart, early in his rule,[3] but it did not last. This makes me think that it might be better to look for a David,[4] with a different heart, instead of a Saul, who really looks impressive. Remember that, for this transition you are searching for a heart, and not a face. There will surely be a difference, in the end.

WISE LEADERS WILL ALWAYS SELECT A DAVID, EVEN THOUGH A SAUL IS REALLY TALL AND HANDSOME.

All this is based on an assumption that you have allowed the "heart of hearts" within your chest to be circumcised by the work of the Holy Spirit. If you have been functioning as a super star, and thus, "larger than life"[5] then you might face a personal struggle, when you install your son in the gospel, which is character challenged. We are not talking about basic honesty, etc., but more about humility and grace. If you feel that you are an elite, then you may be in for some disappointments unless you deal with things now.

PASTOR, HAS YOUR HEART BEEN CIRCUMCISED, OR DO YOU SEE YOURSELF AS AN EXCEPTION … NAUGHTY! NAUGHTY!

Samuel Went in Search of a Heart and Not a Face

The prophet Samuel entered Jesse's camp to sacrifice a heifer[6] to the Lord. In reality, he had come to choose a successor for Saul's throne. On request, Jesse summoned his sons[7] to stand in a column before the prophet for a blessing. Historically, Samuel had occupied the highest office in the land. As a judge, he had anointed Saul to be Israel's first king. Although Samuel had never actually retired, he had backed away from public view, and national responsibilities.

However, in recent days he had felt an urgency to perform one more official service, albeit, as a priestly act. Saul had failed to fulfil his vows to God, which were his "oaths of allegiance,"[8] and was, therefore, disqualified to hold onto his throne. God sent Samuel to the city of Bethlehem and the place where Jesse lived with his family. He requested to see Jesse's family so that he could give his priestly blessing. In the mind of Samuel, however, was the plan to view each of Jesse's sons, while listening to the still small voice of God, for His choice as Saul's successor. It appeared that all the sons of Jesse stood there, from the oldest to the youngest.

Saul bolstered the ratings, but was unable to finish strong ~ we must all learn from the past!

Immediately, upon looking over Jesse's sons, Samuel's eyes fell upon the oldest son, Eliab. The first thought to his mind was, "Surely, the Lord's anointed is before me."[9] It is good that the voice of the Lord, (the voice in his head) chimed in to say, "Whoa, stop... wait a minute. This man cannot be the king. If Eliab were the king, he would become just like the last 'tall guy'[10] you chose." Remember, God had given Saul to be their king, based on their criteria for a king. Yes, God had chosen him, but not based on what Israel needed, but based on their cry, "Give us a king, so that we can be like other nations."

Your Alter Ego is Not Known for Being a Good Judge of Character

It is best, when responding to the voice of the Lord in your life, that you allow the Lord to make the choice for your successor. Do not make the selection based on image, popularity, personality, appearance or IQ. It is not about the flesh, but about issues of the heart and the spirit inside of the man.

DO NOT FASHION YOUR SUCCESSOR AFTER YOUR SCIENTIFIC MIND ON THESE MATTERS ... GOD FORBIDS YOU TO CREATE YOUR VERY OWN FRANKENSTIEN.

If you choose by what would pass the litmus test of your alter ego, then you'll choose according to your flesh's nature. Just because you think this man will make decisions based on your ideals and will reflect your nature better, does not mean the Lord would choose him. God may be willing to give you what you ask for, but, realistically, keep in mind that He sees the bigger picture and is better equipped to make the selection. Remember that God is an intervening God and does not govern "from a distance."[11] God is up close and personal, but too many are not tuned in on the right frequency to detect His presence.

What Does His Heart of Hearts Have in Common with Your Heart of Hearts?

Choose your successor according to whither he is your spiritual son. Have you been his mentor? Does he seem open to learn from you? Does he have your "spiritual DNA?"[12] Of course sometimes leaders choose their own "biological son," because it appears "safe" and is clearly a way of responding to DNA issues, but that may or may not be the best route. Seek the Lord, and ask Him to help you make wise decisions. No one can predict accurately what the next man will do, or what decisions he will make, but there is one thing reasonably sure: If he has no trace of your spiritual DNA then you can be assured that he will eventually, place little value on, or will even betray your wishes and take the work of God in the opposite direction. This is a serious matter and requires counsel and much prayer. You are not infallible and your choices may not be all wise, so ask counsel of the Holy Spirit and others whose judgment you value.

When considering how to recognize spiritual DNA, consider how spiritual relationships and natural comfort zones are put together. Every person, family, club, community, church, region and nation has its own natural inclinations and manner of thinking (aka, hints of DNA). Your church has its own spiritual or social DNA. In the body of Christ there are many streams, or some even call them "tribes." These refer to cultural, and theological leanings influenced by strong personalities from the outset; e.g. different camps like the Faith Movement, Latter Rain, the Prophetic, Seeker sensitive, traditional, etc.

If a leader is chosen from a different stream or tribe, make sure they can be compatible with the culture of your church. Once I was called to pastor a church, which had come into being as a result of a merger of churches from two different denominations. These two groups were from different theological persuasions. It worked out, but proved to be a marriage of complexity.

Finally, choose someone to follow you in leadership, based on whether he is fully aware of the culture of the church, has the same "core values"[13] of the congregation, an awareness and sensitivity of the commitments made through the years by the people, the spiritual personality and leaning of the people and who has a deep personal relationship with God. It is quite necessary that you have a strong personal relationship with him, especially as a mentor. If he cannot receive counsel from you, then you can be assured that he will not be able to receive from you after you become the grandfather of the house.

Some examples of a church's core values are their interest in global evangelization, international missions and civic involvement. If the church has historically had a strong interest and commitment to these areas of ministry, then you can rest assured that it is important to them. If the incoming leadership is prone to nationalism and isolationism (thinking small and in-focused) then there will come a change in policies and even the effectiveness of the church may be at risk. Changes must come slowly. It is also true that some changes are such a clear violation of a church's culture that that church may not survive.

So, after much prayer, be encouraged and choose someone who appreciates your church's history, has a similar, but bigger vision for the future and has a heart large enough to love you.

Introduce Your Joshua or Timothy to Your Ministry Friends

My second mentor was a pastor with whom I worked for five years in the very beginning. He was a mentor with integrity, and certainly his nature was toward generosity and kindness. This pastor was senior to me by fifteen years. I was his assistant pastor, but he introduced my wife and I into the inner core of what ministry was all about. We were able to share the workload of responsibilities and even the social inner circle with those who made up his friends in ministry. It could have been so different, but Pastor BJ Pruitt, over the five years we worked together, made sure I had an up close and personal seat at the table to observe and grow.

We had no less than 100 special guests over those years. I was 21 when I first joined Pastor Pruitt in ministry. He took me on board without regret or hesitation. He never held me at arms length and always made sure that I had everything I needed to embrace the essence of what ministry was all about. He had been a former military officer and understood the zeal of youth, but allowed me to use up my energy, to whatever level I felt, and always without criticism or restraint.

> HE NEVER HELD ME AT ARMS LENGTH, BUT OPENED MY WORLD TO THE ESSENECE OF MINISTRY.

Many of those men and women, who came to minister in his pulpit were of great stature. I was never made to feel like I was on

> PASTOR INCLUDED US EVERY TIME AND HE ALWAYS PAID OUR TAB— THIS IS WHAT I CALL GENEROUS KINDNESS.

the outside looking in, but was always given a seat alongside of them during their times of fellowship. Nearly every guest speaker was treated to a meal in a restaurant. My pastor,[14] and my second mentor, always included Christi and I as he and his wife, Cathy, would host them to dinner, either before the service, or after the service, and often to both. Never, that I can remember, did Pastor Pruitt host them without also including us at the occasion and note this: he always paid for our meal as well as his guests. We never had to hang around and wonder if we'd be asked to the "ball." We were informed that we were "grandfathered in"[15] and would be welcomed to enjoy the moment without feeling the personal insecurity of being left out. Today, after all these years later, I have to say it brings a tear to my eye as I, now more than ever, appreciate the gravity of what he gave me, during those formative years of early ministry.

There were times when I was in my office working and my pastor would stop in, or call me and tell me that an old friend of his was passing through town and wanted to stop in to spend an afternoon, or evening with he and his wife. He would then ask if we had anything planned for the evening? He would then ask if we'd like to meet this old friend of his, and off we'd go to learn more, from a personal friend of his, in an intimate setting where the "greats were gathered." I shall never forget those times.

Pastor Pruitt drew me up and alongside of him so that, as I fellowshipped with he and other senior leaders, I could grow to a mature level long before my time. I learned to think like a senior leader, because of his generous kindness in including me. I shall forever be grateful to this mentor, for he helped turn the lights on to my own passion and ministry. There were valuable lessons, which came to me, as Christi and I sat in restaurants, homes and in the pastor's lounge listening. These lessons often branded my brain with a higher level of understanding and maturity. There were times my wife and I would almost pinch ourselves as we realized what we'd just heard and what we'd just learned. We appreciated the trust and confidence we were able to enjoy during those times.

I have been in ministry, to date, for 47 years. My travels and my times of being guest speaker have extended to so many nations of the world, and to so many churches and to so many pulpits. I have enjoyed the spotlight, the limelight and the golden opportunities extended to me by so many of my pastoral friends.

> SENIOR LEADERS MUST INTRODUCE THEIR JOSHUA OR TIMOTHY TO THEIR SIGNIFICANT FRIENDS IN MINISTRY.

I must say, however, that one of the disappointments I have had over the years is watching senior leaders fail to include, into their inner circle, those they claim to be mentoring. Often they would host the speaker and almost never bring alongside the younger understudy. So many other young leaders are left out in the cold, without clarity or fresh understanding. These young leaders are seldom exposed to the intimate times of discussion, and so they are, too often relegated to remain at the same level, without the opportunity to step up and grow.

This dilemma is like we have all seen, when parents have a social life, but their children are so out of the loop with regards to their parent's friends that they cannot relate even remotely to adults.

Natural life principles include communications between adults and children, children and adults. That is how children grow. Let your child enter occasionally into an adult conversation and he will wise up eventually. So it goes with your understudy. Don't keep him isolated from your friends, give him their address and phone number and encourage him to make a call and have coffee sometime. He'll love you for it, because you are broadening his horizons.

MENTORS INVEST IN LIVES SO THAT THEIR UNDER-STUDY THINKS IN DIFFERENT WAYS.

Young leaders need to have older men in their lives. This means that they need several older men in their lives. They do not just need the mentor who invested most into them, but they need all those the Holy Spirit brings to them. In recent years, I have observed that too often the Joshua or Timothy is not brought into fellowship with older men in ministry, either at times of intimate fellowship, in homes or restaurants, or even as a point of introduction. It is actually the case that the younger understudy has seldom even shaken the hands of any of those who have been a part of the history of the church, as missionaries or guest speakers.

When the senior man takes to dinner the guest speaker, he generally does it alone, with his wife and almost no one else.

* This means that the young stay young in their perspective.

* It means that if the understudy is on a lower level of understanding and experience, and of perspective, he will remain there, until he learns it on his own time and without your help, adding years to his process of growing.

* It also means that the older man is showing a blind spot of personal insensitivity by his failure to give this occasion as a learning time for the younger.

* When pastors include their Joshua/Timothy into their times of fellowship with their friends, there will be some serendipities along the way:

* The pastor gets an added benefit of confirmation as to his choice of this young man as his replacement.

* The pastor gets to see what kind of comments his understudy gives, thereby confirming his own suspicions regarding the level of his choice for the future and how he fits in.

* And he will have made a new friend, not just a colleague in ministry.

Sometimes the Joshua or Timothy is in another part of the building involved in other facets of ministry every time the guests come and the years pass, without any exposure of any kind. And then the day comes for transitions to be made and the baton is passed without any contact with those senior leaders. I realize that these are momentous days, and that there may be a gulf between the "Baby Boomer generation" and those who make up the future leaders of today's church. I also realize that my generation, as well as the generation of the current mentors may be vastly different from what the church will become. Granted, I also may not be aware of a developing blind spot, which may be in the minds of the current leaders.

> PASTORS CAN
> HAVE BLIND
> SPOTS LIKE
> ANYONE ELSE.

* Could it be that senior leaders do not introduce their understudies to those senior men, who are their friends, because they themselves were never exposed to the mentors I have enjoyed?

41

- Could it be that these senior leaders see only the benefits they can give to the Joshua, and do not see the benefits of other "older leaders," and so may be short circuiting the values, which should be embraced by the younger man?

- Is it possible that he feels insecure of his own past relationships and is now trying to give the young guy a chance to make much younger friends, thereby shutting out history?

- Is it possible that some of these leaders feel that history is irrelevant and it must bow out and go away?

- Note: Much can be learned from history and care must be taken to build strong bridges to connect the past to the future.

- Observation: The current times can often be seen as a canyon of treacherous travel. The past is clear and the future is still to be made, so a bridge is just the thing to help make smooth the journey.

This book, "Is there a Grandfather in the House?" has been written hoping for the ear of leaders to be awakened. Awakened to how you are to handle the transitions, which you face in the future. It is also written with the hope that you will see how you could do it all better.

Do you know the "heart of hearts" of your Joshua or Timothy? It may do you good to host your mentee to times of communing with older men, under your observation. This way you may discover that he is wiser than you think, and can step up and take the baton of leadership. You hold the key as to how well adjusted he is becoming.

Endnotes

1. www.chabad.org/library/article_cdo/aid/812861/jewish/A-Pillow-Full-of-Feathers.htm ~ A Pillow Full of Feathers By Shoshannah Brombacher

2. www.waywordradio.org/train_wreck ~ train wreck n. a disaster or failure, especially one that is unstoppable or unavoidable; a disorganized, problematic, or chaotic person or thing; an incongruous situation. (source: Double-Tongued Dictionary)

3. I Samuel 10:9-11 NLT "As Saul turned and started to leave, God gave him a new heart, and all Samuel's signs were fulfilled that day. When Saul and his servant arrived at Gibeah, they saw a group of prophets coming toward them. Then the Spirit of God came powerfully upon Saul, and he, too, began to prophesy. When those who knew Saul heard about it, they exclaimed, "What? Is even Saul a prophet? How did the son of Kish become a prophet?"

4. Ron Bishop wrote his Research Thesis, when completing his Bachelor of Theology Degree, with International Bible College, San Antonio, Texas, USA, entitled: "Saul and David – Man's Choice and God's Choice" – In this thesis emphasis is based on a look at the 'Heart of Hearts', which existed within the lives of these two leaders.

5. www.yourdictionary.com/larger-than-life ~ adj. "The definition of larger than life is someone or something that is so special, famous, well known or important that it takes on an image of being greater than others of is kind." This has more to do with a person's self-image and less to do with reality. Certainly all need to keep their self-image intact, but the downside is the study of narcissism.

6. I Samuel 16:2-3 NLT "But Samuel asked, 'How can I do that? If Saul hears about it he will kill me.' 'Take a heifer with you,' the Lord replied, 'and say that you have come to make a sacrifice to the Lord. Invite Jesse to the sacrifice, and I will show you which of his sons to anoint for me.'"

7. 1 Chronicles 2:13-16 AMP "Jesse became the father of Eliab his firstborn, Abinadab the second, Shimea the third, Nethanel the fourth, Raddai the fifth, Ozem the sixth, David the seventh. Their sisters were Zeruiah and Abigail. The sons of Zeruiah: Abishai, Joab, and Asahel, three."

8. en.wikipedia.org/wiki/Oath_of_allegiance ~Sometimes called, Oaths of Office. "An oath of allegiance is an oath whereby a subject or citizen acknowledges a duty of allegiance and swears loyalty to monarch or country."

9. 1 Samuel 16:6 MSG When they arrived, Samuel took one look at Eliab and thought, "Here he is! God's anointed!"

10. I Samuel 9:2 TLB "His son Saul was the most handsome man in Israel. And he was head and shoulders taller than anyone else in the land!"

11. www.songfacts.com/detail.php?id=4273 ~ The song, **"From a Distance,"** was written by Julie Gold, but recorded by Bette Midler. "This was written by singer/songwriter Julie Gold, who was working odd jobs in New York to make ends meet when she received a very special 30th birthday gift from her parents back home in Philadelphia: the piano she had played as a child. The men who delivered her piano told her that it had gotten pretty cold in the truck on its way to her, and that she shouldn't play it for a day to give it time to adjust to its new surroundings in her apartment. Gold wanted to play it very badly, but, not wanting to cause damage, resisted the urge. Instead, she just "hugged it and polished it." The next day, she sat down at that piano and wrote this song in about 2 hours. In our interview with Julie Gold, she said, "I only set out to write a decent song about the difference between the way things seem and the way things are." However, many people interpret this song to mean that God governs the earth, but does so from a great distance, estranged from the necessary closeness and care we need so much. My thoughts are that God is always nearby and available to us.

12. dictionary.reference.com/browse/dna ~ Genetic DNA is for the human body, but "spiritual DNA" is involving the "Body of Christ" as well as such things as culture and relationships. For example, as this source states: "Nongenetic traits, qualities, or features that characterize a person or thing."

13. humanresources.about.com/od/glossaryc/g/Core-Values.htm?utm_term=church ~ **"Core Values are What you Believe"** ~ "Core values are traits or qualities that you consider not just worthwhile, they represent an individual's or organization's highest priorities, deeply held beliefs, and core, fundamental driving forces."

14. My first mentor was my Father, Earl Daniel Bishop (Born: 1930 -Passed: 2000). My best way to describe my Dad is that he was "John Wayne," but a man who had a serious prayer life. I must say that he was my first hero and remains so today. He taught me to be a man.

15. "Grandfathered in" ~ means that there will be no discussion about whether we were invited to join in with the guests. We always had been invited and we were never left out. We were a part of the party.

Chapter 6

RESPONDING TO THE CALL

THE CALL, UNCTION, OBEDIENCE

Wͪhen an individual is divinely called by the Holy Spirit to enter into special service for the Kingdom of God, it is so different than just being inclined to follow a particular profession or vocation. To have the natural affinity to become a nurse, architect, doctor or lawyer, may be strong in its own way; but to experience a powerful vision or epiphany,[1] which "brands your brain"[2] and reorders your thinking, where you decide to become a minister of the Gospel, is something else all together.

Many church leaders experienced a divine visitation, which left them recognizing that they were being challenged to set their house in order, for service to God and the Church. This visitation made all the difference in how they spent their life currency. Those who have never met with such a "Damascus experience"[3] may not have considered the significant impact it can have on the persona[4] or future plans of an individual. This impact became evident in the greetings and conversation of the Apostle Paul as he referred to himself as a "servant of Jesus Christ,"[5] "a devoted slave of Jesus Christ"[6] and a "Prisoner for the sake of Jesus Christ."[7] We can clearly see a difference in Saul[8] and Paul.[9]

What is it that changes in the worldview and paradigm of the one who experiences this call? Everything.

The question always remains the same. Will this man, or woman who receives this call, remain committed, compliant and accountable to the inner workings of the Holy Spirit? Only time and eternity will tell the full story. In the meantime, God has enlisted another member of His "special forces"[10] to work with mankind and to build His church.[11]

The call, which a man of God experiences, will require deep commitments and a rearrangement of priorities. In this case, it involves more than our earthly lives. It is necessary to have a deep and very strong belief in Jesus Christ and the significance of eternity. Earthly and temporal realms are only for our natural lifespan, whereas the Kingdom of God is for eternity. Every person has an eternal soul. When the Holy Spirit places a call upon an individual, it is to serve; it is not about prominence, reputation, career or accomplishments. It is about "Plundering hell to populate heaven."[12] Every soul is important and must hear the "Good News" of the Kingdom, so they can make a decision to receive Christ.

> YOUR FLESH WILL LIVE FOR THIS LIFE, YOUR SOUL WILL LIVE FOR ETERNITY.

The Prophet Jeremiah received the call[13] and was commissioned to go to the nation. The force he felt was so formidable that he actually described it as "fire shut up in my bones."[14] The word of God was so powerful, within that he felt it impossible to hold back.

When Your Call Becomes a Mandate[15]

Mandate–A requirement that something be done.

In the beginning, that wooing of the Holy Spirit is seen as a call. This call gives new meaning, new purpose and new clarity to the value and purpose of you life. It causes you to take constant inventory of what you want to do and where you want to go, so that you do not miss your times of visitation, which come at various intervals all through your life. If your life remains in good order, that time of visitation will be to challenge you and draw you out of your realm and into His realm. It will make you more aware of the Kingdom of God within you.

ACCEPTING DIVINE ASSIGNMENTS IS A MATURE RESPONSE TO YOUR CALL, BUT A MANDATE IS A HIGHER LEVEL IN ITSELF.

As the call of God matures in your life, you will discover that you become aware of new opportunities and new assignments, or a personal commission. These new doors slowly become brighter and align with your gifts and appetites. You find, by these new alignments clarity to the point that you begin to embrace the fact that "I can do that," although often you will face challenges you cannot do without the help of the Holy Spirit. These things may not always progress into a personal mandate, but often it does. Your mandate just may open for you new and unique doors, and visa versa. The short of it all, is that you will find personal satisfaction and joy by applying your energies to the call, plus the open doors, plus what may become your mandate.

When you receive a "call" into Christian service, it does not mean you have rank as an officer in God's military. If compared to a military environment, you would initially only achieve something like "Private status," as a Junior-enlisted employee of the US Army. You are not an officer, and are certainly non-commissioned. When you receive your assignment to pastor, or to teach, etc. then you may rise to non-commissioned status, and only rise higher (just as a matter of giving clarity) as you mature in your obedience and your effectiveness. It all depends on you and the level to which you become responsible. You may be able to achieve non-commission officer status, as your value to the Kingdom increases. The hope or the ideal is that you, at some point will receive a commission and become recognized by the mandate, which involves more than a specific assignment. The main difference is whether you are commissioned or non-commissioned. When you receive a "mandate," which will alter your life plan significantly, then you will surely achieve a greater rank, although humility still rules the day for you as a "servant leader."[16]

Your mandate will lay at your door more than a temporary assignment. Let me say that, for me, one of my mandates is to write my thoughts for posterity in books and blogs. When you feel the call, then later, as you mature in that call, and discover the feeling of a personal mandate, then you are ascending to a place of reality where you understand more about yourself and you know more about where you're going and why you are going there. At this point in time, I am involved in making radio broadcasts for the local Irish area, where we live. I do not see this as a mandate, but rather as an open door to walk through to impact the area as much as I can, given the fact that I have the open door and the relationship with those who operate the station. Only time will prove whether it will progress into a personal mandate. At this time it is an assignment. As time passes you will discover the most valuable questions and answers about things, and your mandate will help you to help others prepare for their own times of visitation.

My Personal Story On the Call

I was 12 years old, and my entire family had been Christians now, for all of six months. I was sitting on the third row, the end seat next to the middle isle at a church in my childhood hometown of Bristol, Virginia/Tennessee. The pastor of the church had just begun to speak, as he was delivering his message to the congregation on that Sunday evening. The building was just big enough to accommodate about 200 people. As I sat there, taking in the service, something took place, which changed my life forever. I found myself seeing a vision, which transported me from that building to another building, which I had never seen before. It was a narrow wooden structure, about 15 feet wide and about 40 feet long. This was a small church building, seating only about 35 people, and with a small platform. My dad was standing on the platform. He was a new Christian at the time of my vision, and had never stood on a church platform, so this was note worthy to me. It was especially interesting when I heard him say, in the vision, "Tonight, I am not going to preach. My son, Ron, is going to minister for us." He then stepped aside and I stood up, a full-grown man. The vision was finished and I was drawn back into that same church where I had been sitting initially.

> JUST LIKE THE PROPHET ISAIAH, I HAD A VISION WHILE SITTING IN CHURCH ... AMAZING.

Time passed, I became an adult, and began traveling and preaching in churches around the nation. My dad had followed through in his own call and was now, also preaching in churches in the mid-west.

49

I came to visit my family. My dad invited me to a service he was leading and asked me to speak that evening. When we arrived, the building was a narrow wooden structure, and seated about 35 people. Dad asked me to sit on the platform, and to speak that evening. I recognized nothing. He then said to the congregation: "Tonight, I am not going to preach. My son, Ron, is going to minister for us." As he stepped aside, I stood up. The feeling of déjà vu hit me in the chest so powerfully. I knew instantly that this was the place I'd seen in my vision, eight years earlier, at age 12. Now, again at age 20, I was clearly aware of a powerful and divine call upon my life.

The call of God is a valid experience, although not experienced by everyone.[17] I cannot speak for every minister of the Gospel, but I feel, privileged, to have been called into the ministry.[18] Those who have experienced this type of call, find themselves, making a lifetime commitment to the call. This becomes one of the reasons they do not easily step back from it, even when they get older.

Endnotes

1. www.merriam-webster.com/dictionary ~epiphany: "a moment in which you suddenly see or understand something in a new or very clear way."

2. "Branding the Brain" ~ idiom coined by Ron Bishop re: telling Bible stories in such a way as to impact the mind on the profound and life changing effect of these stories.

3. The story of Saul's meeting with Jesus while en route to Damascus: Acts 9:3-7

4. www.merriam-webster.com/dictionary ~persona: "the way you behave, talk, etc., with other people that causes them to see you as a particular kind of person; the image or personality that a person presents to other people."

5. Romans 1:1 KJV "Paul, a servant of Jesus Christ..."

6. Romans 1:1 MSG "I, Paul, am a devoted slave of Jesus Christ on assignment, authorized as an apostle to proclaim God's words and acts..."

7. Philemon 1:1 MSG "I, Paul, am a prisoner for the sake of Christ..."

8. Take note of the personality and nature of Saul of Tarsus in Acts 8:1-3 and 9:1-2

9. The Apostle Paul was originally called, Saul, which was his Hebrew name. After his conversion to Christ, he experienced a call to the Gentiles. Because of this, he chose to be called by his Greek name, Paul, as it was more acceptable to the people he would meet. Saul's conversion was so dramatic he was essentially a different man anyway.

10. In the Old Testament, we see David and his Mighty Men (2 Samuel 23)

11. Matthew 16:18 "... upon this Rock I will build my church; and the gates of hell shall not prevail against it."

12. "Plundering hell to populate heaven" ~ Reinhard Bonnke's theme of ministry. His ministry is called CFAN, or Christ For All Nations and is based in Hamburg, Germany.

13. Jeremiah received his Call, and his first commission is documented in Jeremiah 1:4-10

14. Jeremiah 20:9 NKJV Then I said, "I will not make mention of Him, nor speak anymore in His name. But His word was in my heart like a burning fire shut up in my bones; I was weary of holding it back, and I could not."

15. Define the term: Mandate – A requirement that something be done; a mandate is the authority to do a particular thing that is needed; An official order, or commission to do something; Required action, or purpose as to make happen what is needed.

16. index.about.com/index?q=Ranks+in+US+Army+in+Order&qs rc=6&o=22825&l=sem&qo=relatedSearchNarrow

17. 1 Corinthians 1:25-27 NLT "This foolish plan of God is wiser than the wisest of human plans, and God's weakness is stronger than the greatest of human strength. Remember, dear brothers and sisters, that few of you were wise in the world's eyes or powerful or wealthywhen God called you. Instead, God chose things the world considers foolish in order to shame those who think they are wise. And he chose things that are powerless to shame those who are powerful."

18. I Timothy 1:12 NKJV "And I thank Christ Jesus our Lord who has enabled me, because He counted me faithful, putting me into the ministry."

Chapter 7

GRANDFATHERS WILL BE TESTED

FAILING IS NOT AN OPTION

Grandfather is "the father of one's father, or mother."[1] "The person who founded or originated something."[2]

Grandfathers are a phenomenon and a valuable part of society. I realize that times are changing and the world is becoming a different place in which to live. Someone said, "This is not our grandfather's world (nor our father's, for that matter)."[3] We need grandfathers so that we do not lose a sense of history, or the perspective, which he brings to us on issues of the heart as well as valuable lessons not to be forgotten. When we think of grandfather, we think of honesty and wisdom, genuineness and simplicity. The worldview of "simpler days," when things were not so complicated, can also add a dash of reality.

On our subject of leadership and transition, we see that, as the leader or set man of the church advances in years he is faced with choices he has never faced before. He has been relevant, proactive and engaged with all the age groups and diverse demographics of his congregation. He has shown a genuine interest in the personal challenges of so many of the members of his parish, and yet now faces the inevitable passing of the baton to someone else, who must take on those responsibilities, and all from the paradigms of a changing world, to a changed congregation.

In some ways this transition is like having birthed a baby, and now, like Jochebed, Moses' mother, choosing to yield it to someone else who is as diverse as Pharaoh's daughter.[4] The difference is that, you have worked a long time and have grown this "baby" up, to where your congregation is now quite adult.

Thoughts that may go through your mind are with regard to your ability to transfer authority to another. Your love for the people is great, and at times, you may feel like such transitions are a little like going through bereavement or even like walking through a minefield. Another question you may encounter is whether the faithful will be able to accept the new guy; will they willingly embrace him? Will we loose parishioners? Will they cross this bridge to their future? At times you've seen yourself as inflexible, and you are suspicious that the sheep that follow you, are much the same.

UNDERSTAND THE PAST, AND YOU'LL MASTER THE FUTURE. LOOK ONLY TO THE FUTURE AND THE PAST WILL THROW YOU A CURVE!

The roles of grandfathers and grandmothers are designed in the heart of our creator, to aid society in dealing with perspectives on history and the future. For the first couple millenniums mankind did not rely on written history, as much as it did on the passing down of oral history. Today society does not lend

54

itself as much to having a strong understanding of history, or clarity on what we will face in decades to come, as much as it does on understanding current events and the dominant local and national culture. Grandfathers will help you with the past, and by that, you'll gain perspective on just what may come in the future. Most agree that a grandparent will help understand what exactly happened and why. If we understand the past, then it stands to reason that we may be able to avoid the same pitfalls in the future. This would be a good time to call out, "Is there a grandfather in the house?"

The following are just a few of the things a grandfather will bring to life for the current generation; an understanding of right and wrong, moral values, the value of commitments, your word is your bond, faithfulness, falling in love for a lifetime, keeping confidence when counselling, praying for a blessing over the day, and for the meal before you.

Grandfathers in leadership roles, can slip up, fail, destroy their clout, or squander their "Grandfather currency."

Remember, You are a Grandfather, Not "The Daddy"

I accompanied an ordained chaplain who was working in a specialized ministry. It was only the second time I was meeting his pastor. I was introducing a European minister to these two men. However, I was underwhelmed[5] by the demeanor of the senior pastor, who took it upon himself to discipline and verbally correct the chaplain on keeping a prompt schedule. He did all this before even giving us greeting and without, even a question, as to the reasons for the twenty-minutes of tardiness. I was tempted to come to the chaplain's defence, but was happy to see that; no facial distress was visible in his eyes, except for a bit of embarrassment. That senior minister suffered a great loss of respect and "grandfather currency" on that day. He had overdrawn his account with everyone in the room. To this point he has not regained it. Note, that he was not the younger man's employer, supervisor, or overseer. He was recognized, by the chaplain, respectfully as his chosen pastor, but acted like the daddy. This was not the time, the place, nor the manner for such confrontation. My wife would say, "bad form."

Grandparents Should Not Tell Their Children How to Parent

"Grandparents should not tell their children how to raise the grandchildren,"[6] and grandfathers must not tell the pastor how to run the church. Allow them to make their own mistakes, or to show you that they just may know what they're doing. Remember that your son in the Gospel was designed for this role. You are now equipped to be a grandfather of the church, and he is better equipped to be the father in the church. He is the one with the authority, and you are in a supportive role; so support you must.

> OFTEN DISAGREEMENTS COME TO A HEAD BECAUSE SOMEONE USES EMAILS, OR SOCIAL MEDIA ... WHICH CAN BE AS DANGEROUS AS USING A SWORD.

Our ministry has taken us to nearly eighty nations on six continents, with legal residency in six nations on three continents. As a result of having many friends and acquaintances in about 100 nations, we have seen "The Good, the Bad and the Ugly."[7] Our experiences just might blow the mind of many. We have overheard conversations, and we have seen indiscretions, which have almost made my head hurt. I have seen emails, which would bring empires down, and I am aware of words being said, which leave hearts and lives broken, possibly even going so far as to render a "Grandfather wound."

In many situations all the parties are right, and all are wrong; in the end nobody is happy, and all are offended. I have seen lots of drama, loads of debate, and yet there was no resolution and relationships were defiled. Often prideful comments travel across state lines, national boundaries, and, because of toxic attitudes, are almost strong enough for Homeland Security to get involved. I must call such situations a dismal failure.

If we fail in our spiritual role, then we also flunk the test in the bigger responsibility. I sometimes ask, "What was he thinking?" A common reality is that "you can win the battle and lose the war."[8] Life is too short, and the end too close for us to fail the test in any of these contests of life. Please, remember the Golden Rule and "do unto others as you'd have them do unto you." Do not take offence at every offensive statement. Turn the other cheek and lose once in a while. Allowing yourself to lose occasionally will help you deal with your need for humility. And for heaven's sake, please take your medication, and if the dosage is too weak, or too strong, go back to your doctor, or ask for prayer.

Being a Godly Role Model is Central

One huge challenge is not so much being a modern grandparent, as being a Biblical grandfather, or a Biblical grandmother.

A grandfather must display the nature of Christ, whenever possible. I realize that we all have good days and bad days, but, for the most part, we don't get a pass. We must pass the test all the time. So, be diligent and show the younger, the way, by leading down the right path. Try to do the right thing, even if it is not popular. Here is a principle to keep in mind: "The right thing is not always popular, and the popular thing is not always right."[9]

Talk Less and Listen More

"More is caught than taught and your words will be drowned out by what you do. You might say one thing, but then do another. Such actions, communicate that being a hypocrite is okay. When they see you do the right thing and that it matches what you say, then that is one powerful lesson that will be passed on and on and on."[10]

So, be strong and keep the faith of our fathers, for the sake of this and future generations. We are advancing toward a potentially dark future, and you are carrying the Christian banner, which encourages all of us to stay with righteous coordinates, so that this mighty ship will continue onward to a positive and a Godly end.

Endnotes

1. www.merriam-webster.com/dictionary/grandfather

2. www.oxforddictionaries.com/definition/english/grandfather

3. www.thedailybeast.com/articles/ReaderPollReports-NSA

4. Exodus 2:1-10 Birth of Moses to Amram and Jochebed, launching the baby

5. www.merriam-webster.com/dictionary/whelmed ~ whelmed: to turn (as a dish or vessel) upside down usually to cover something. Response would be In "Neutral." Overwhelmed: to cause to have too many things to deal with. Response would be in "Overdrive." Underwhelmed: to fail to impress or stimulate." Note: Lots of things whelm us, few things overwhelm us, but even fewer things underwhelm us. Response would be "Reverse."

6. www.whatchristianswanttoknow.com ~ What Is The Role of a Christian Grandfather or Grandmother?

7. The 1966 Italian epic, Spaghetti Western, Movie: "The Good, the Bad and the Ugly… with Clint Eastwood. It was a co-production between companies in Italy, Spain, West Germany and the United States. The characters were Good, they were Bad and they were Ugly. My wife says it should have been named, "The Ugly, the Uglier and the Ugliest."

8. answers.yahoo.com/question ~ "you can win the battle and lose the war." ~ Means that you won a particular point in an argument but lost the argument itself. Can be applied to multiple scenarios, not just arguments.

9. www.whatchristianswanttoknow.com ~ What Is The Role of a Christian Grandfather or Grandmother?

10. www.whatchristianswanttoknow.com ~ What Is The Role of a Christian Grandfather or Grandmother?

Is There a Grandfather in the House?

Chapter 8

SIGNIFICANT MENTORS AND THEIR INFLUENCE

NICODEMUS AND GAMALIEL

The term, mentoring, has been around since the days of Greek Mythology.[1] Simply defined it is "a wise and trusted counselor or teacher, or an influential senior sponsor or supporter."[2] "Mentoring is to support and encourage people to manage their own learning in order that they may maximize their potential, develop their skills, improve their performance and become the person they want to be. It is a partnership between two people (mentor and mentoree) normally working in a similar field or sharing similar experiences. It is a helpful relationship based upon mutual trust and respect."[3]

There are two Hebrew scholars in the New Testament, who have been admired, albeit from a distance. One is Nicodemus[4] and the second is Gamaliel.[5] Both were wise men, Pharisees, and teachers. Both have been respected within the Christian circle, because of the level of wisdom they both displayed in the days when Jesus was in Israel.

Nicodemus was hungry and inquisitive. He was a Jewish Rabbi and became a friend of Jesus. He was a rich man, a ruler, a Pharisee, and a member of the Sanhedrin.[6] He was curious as to the credibility of this young teacher. Driven by this curiosity he came, under cover of darkness, to learn from Jesus. The biggest lesson he seems to have learned was of the new birth.[7] Now, after the crucifixion, Nicodemus[8] came, but this time, during the day, accompanying Joseph of Arimathea,[9] to bring 75 pounds of spices and ointments for Jesus' burial.[10] Here we have an interesting picture of two prominent members of the Sanhedrin, the highest Jewish counsel; and the very court, which had condemned Jesus to death, coming to attend to his burial. On this second visit to Jesus, they clearly were not avoiding daylight, nor in fear of being discovered. They were quite willing to make a public statement of their commitment to the young Jewish rabbi, now dead at only 33 years of age.

Nearly everyone who knows much of Paul's story has heard of his mentor, Gamaliel.[11] Gamaliel was the head of the rabbinical school, where Saul/Paul learned as a young man.[12] Most have heard of Gamaliel's wisdom and have appreciated how he spoke up for the persecuted disciples.[13] They may not know a lot about him, but they will think of him in good light as a teacher who taught logic and wisdom[14] to the man who would become known as Paul, the Apostle.

GAMALIEL SPOKE UP TO PROTECT THE APOSTLES WHEN THEY WERE AT RISK.

Both Nicodemus and Gamaliel were first learners, then teachers, and devout in they're relationships with God. In history it is said that Gamaliel's grandson became a Christian.[15] Both Nicodemus and Gamaliel became mentors and helped younger men find their way.

The life of a Christian leader can take on many turns and involve varied assignments. As you get older the options narrow to fewer choices. Add to the natural limitations, societal changes and your later years can get complicated. If you, as a leader can redefine yourself, and consider reaching out to young leaders, the Holy Spirit can multiply your options. Young men are often hungry to listen, and quite willing to take time to learn. But, they will not give much time to small talk; they want solid wisdom and powerful influences in their lives. This generation wants to make their mark and build a vibrant and viable work for God.

YOUNG MEN ARE HUNGRY TO LISTEN AND GLAD TO LEARN, BUT AREN'T INTERESTED IN SMALL TALK.

If you will prayerfully strategize, as a Christian leader, and seek God's help in your march toward the future, then you will find that mentoring will give you value and significance. This is not about getting up a load of sons for grandfathers to mentor, but for the grandfathers to be given a wakeup call, so they do not think their assignments are finished.

The day will come for us all when we will give account of what we have done during our lifetimes. We do not want Jesus to say, "you did well, my son, you did a good work, but you kept hold of your assignment too long; and kept your sons in a box, when they were raring to go to become fathers in their own right. Your assignment, as pastor, lasted 50 years and your son only had time to eek out 25, because you did not allow him to "grow up." You thought it was about you; however, my son, it was all about me,[16] and what I'd do through you, as my vessel of honor. You thought they were just little boys. You taught him, and taught him, you showed him, and then showed him again, and finally you branded him an Absalom when he grew impatient, could not handle your indecisiveness any longer, and ran away to start the work I was burning in his heart. He was also called; and you lost a great opportunity, and in the end; you felt abandoned, disappointed, and betrayed. It was not necessary. If you'd just realized your own "seasons of life" and your own mortality, then I could have used you as a "wise old man, a sage, a grandfather."

The Bert Brisbane Story

Now I want to tell you a successful mentoring story. Pastor Albert "Bert" Brisbane was a pioneer in San Francisco, CA, which was then, and is still a very difficult part of the world for the expansion of Christianity. As beautiful as San Francisco is, it is also, like so many of the larger cities of the world, not without its own unique challenges. Bert was blessed to have strong and committed people join alongside of him to assist him in holding up his arms during those times.[17]

He founded and established a church in 1952 with their first services held in the home of two fully committed friends, Melvin and Ellen Johnson.[18] They were there from the beginning, and remain strong supporters 63 years later with Cornerstone Church. The comment Melvin made to Bert was, "If you will start the church, we'll back you all the way." I met the Johnsons in July of 1979, while ministering for Pastor Brisbane and the church, there in San Francisco.

In the beginning, with creativity and hard work they secured the present building and paid for it, largely through the bus driving occupation of Bert Brisbane. Often, it is said, that he was so busy that he would invite those on the church's leadership team to come along with him on a complimentary bus ride to have their business meetings. Somehow they would take care of church decisions as they rode along his city bus route. Interestingly, they could gain a free ride on his bus by saying the secret password: "Geronimo."

The years passed and Bert looked for his successor. He was amazed when he saw a strong interest in his young grandson, Terry Brisbane. Terry was a University student, and coordinated his studies and the mentoring times he enjoyed with his delightful grandfather. Here are some descriptive comments, which have come down to us. Melvin said, "Bert had a big booming voice. When he spoke, even to a handful of people, he did so like he was talking to 300." One comment was that, "Pastor Brisbane reminded me of a Christian version of John Wayne."[19]

One day, when Terry was about the age of 25 his grandfather called him and asked him to stop by the church. He had something he wanted to talk about. When Terry came into his office, his grandfather handed him a note, which said:

"Thanks for the memories. Adios"

Then he said, "The church is yours, Terry. You are now the pastor. I am moving to Chico, CA. He moved that week to Chico. That may seem, for obvious reasons, a bit abrupt, but it just may be how John Wayne[20] would have made the transfer.

WE COULD NOT DO TODAY, IF GRANDDAD HAD NOT SAVED YESTERDAY.

Although Cornerstone Church has made many improvements over the years, they still honor Bert Brisbane and the early parishioners for their hard work in securing the original property and building, which remain such a blessing today. In San Francisco properties are almost "impossible to find," and the prices are some of the highest in the world. They have one of the largest congregations in all of San Francisco. The two campuses have five services on the weekend, with the second campus being called the Lake Merced campus. Those who attend, as well as the staff, call Terry simply "PT." If you visit the church you'll find them real and down to earth, with no "religious spirits" hanging out.

One strong point, which Bert Brisbane brought into reality, is his tenacity for investing in and securing the future for the work he was establishing. The fact is: You may build a strong church or congregation, but if you fail to take steps to give them assets or tools, then the vision may suffer a set back. This is where this mighty warrior showed extreme gifting and strength.

Often Leaders are Afraid Their Sons will Wreck the Car

When our son, Cameron, was in his early twenties we took a drive in my car. As we left the house I tossed him the keys and said, "Cameron, you drive." This surprised him. He smiled and said, "Sure." Then he drove with a smile on his face. Something happened that day. He could sense a trust between us. The years passed and I had often given him the keys. Then there came a point when I was dealing with something, and I needed to get a second opinion. I gave him a call, explained my concerns, and asked him for advice. I was amazed at how he gave me "rock solid" counsel. Now, I see my son as one of my mentors. This has changed our relationship again.

The reason older men don't like to allow their sons to step up and actually drive is they're afraid they will wreck the car. So, when their sons become men they keep the keys close to their hearts so they can maintain control. The real issue here is trust. Control issues are not what matters to grandfathers. Grandfathers are aware that they don't need as much as before. They have come to realize that they have more years behind them than they have ahead of them.

It is vitally important, as you grow through the stages of your life, that you step from one chapter into the next. Why would any of us want to stay in the first chapter of our life-book? Life has so many opportunities and so many doors. If you are to live it to the full, then you must step through the doors, which God opens to you.

Young men, today you may not see all the value of his wit and wisdom, but the day will come when your mentor is gone and you will be grateful for what you learned from him and will find yourself quoting him frequently. Actually, you will be certified by whom you sat under, as Saul sat under Gamaliel.

Endnotes

1. Wikipedia.org/wiki/mentor

2. dictionary.reference.com/browse/MENTOR

3. mentorset.org.uk/pages/mentoring.htm

4. John 3:1,4,9 Nicodemus came to learn of Jesus.

5. Acts 5:34-39 & Acts 22:3 Gamaliel a mentor & teacher of Saul of Tarsus

6. latter-rain.com/ltrain/nicod.htm

7. John 3:1-21, especially: 3-7 NLT - "Jesus replied, 'I tell you the truth, unless you are born again, you cannot see the Kingdom of God.' 'What do you mean?' exclaimed Nicodemus. 'How can an old man go back into his mother's womb and be born again?' Jesus replied, 'I assure you; no one can enter the Kingdom of God without being born of water and the Spirit. Humans can reproduce only human life, but the Holy Spirit gives birth to spiritual life. So don't be surprised when I say, 'You must be born again.'"

8. Christianity.about.com/od/newtestamentpeople/a/Nicodemus.htm - "Every seeker has a deep feeling that there must be something more to life, a great truth to be discovered. That was the case with Nicodemus, who came to Jesus Christ at night because he suspected this young teacher might be the Messiah promised to Israel by God."

9. Christianity.about.com/od/newtestamentpeople/a/Joseph-Of-Arimathea.htm - Joseph of Arimathea - Donor of Jesus' Tomb. Following Jesus Christ has always been dangerous, but it was especially so for Joseph of Arimathea. He was a prominent member of the Sanhedrin, the court, which condemned Jesus to death. Joseph risked his reputation and his life by standing up for Jesus, but his faith far outweighed his fear.

10. John 19:38-40 NLT "Afterward Joseph of Arimathea, who had been a secret disciple of Jesus (because he feared the Jewish leaders), asked Pilate for permission to take down Jesus' body. When Pilate gave permission, Joseph came and took the body away. With him came Nicodemus, the man who had come to Jesus at night. He brought about seventy-five pounds of perfumed ointment made from myrrh and aloes. Following Jewish burial custom, they wrapped Jesus' body with the spices in long sheets of linen cloth."

11. en.wikipedia.org/wiki/Gamaliel - Sometimes called, Gamaliel the Elder. He was both a member of the Sanhedrin and considered a "leading authority in the Sanhedrin in the early 1st century CE."

12. Paul reminds King Agrippa, in Acts 26:4 MSG, of how he grew up and was trained in the way of the "Pharisee, the most demanding branch of our religion."

13. Acts 5:25-40, especially comments by Gamaliel: 33-39 NLT "When they heard this, the high council was furious and decided to kill them. But one member, a Pharisee named Gamaliel, who was an expert in religious law and respected by all the people, stood up and ordered that the men be sent outside the council chamber for a while. Then he said to his colleagues, 'Men of Israel, take care what you are planning to do to these men! Some time ago there was that fellow Theudas, who pretended to be someone great. About 400 others joined him, but he was killed, and all his followers went their various ways. The whole movement came to nothing. After him, at the time of the census, there was Judas of Galilee. He got people to follow him, but he was killed, too, and all his followers were scattered. So my advice is, leave these men alone. Let them go. If they are planning and doing these things merely on their own, it will soon be overthrown. But if it is from God, you will not be able to overthrow them. You may even find yourselves fighting against God!'"

14. It is worthy of note in Acts 5:34-40, that Gamaliel defused the volatile situation by requesting the Apostles step out of the room, where the high counsel was meeting, and then gave a caution to them to be very careful, lest they find themselves fighting against God. Note that he was able to move the rhetoric from "When they heard this, the high council was furious and decided to kill them..." to "The others accepted his advice. They called in the apostles and had them flogged. Then they ordered them never again to speak in the name of Jesus, and they let them go. The apostles left the high council rejoicing that God had counted them worthy to suffer disgrace for the name of Jesus. And every day, in the Temple and from house to house, they continued to teach and preach this message: 'Jesus is the Messiah'." So, here we see that Gamaliel actually saved the lives of the Apostles that day. Too little has been said about his influence that day.

15. en.wikipedia.org/wiki/Gamaliel – Gamaliel's granddaughter married a priest named Simon ben Nathanael. In Christian tradition, their second son Abibo converted to Christianity.

16. The church, the Kingdom of God and all of creation is *all about God* and what He planned, from the beginning. *It is not about you.* He is the Potter and we are the clay, pure and simple. If we follow His plan, then we will discover that, if you make your life assignment, about doing "The will of the Father," then you will have a super-fantastic legacy to enjoy.

17. Exodus 17:10-13 MSG "Joshua did what Moses ordered in order to fight Amalek. And Moses, Aaron, and Hur went to the top of the hill. It turned out that whenever Moses raised his hands, Israel was winning, but whenever he lowered his hands, Amalek was winning. But Moses' hands got tired. So they got a stone and set it under him. He sat on it and Aaron and Hur held up his hands, one on each side. So his hands remained steady until the sun went down. Joshua defeated Amalek and its army in battle."

18. Melvin & Ellen Johnson have been missionaries in a number of countries for many years. Having worked with United Airlines for 37 years, he retired in 1990. For a number of years they were associated with Evangel Bible Translators and its CEO Syvelle Phillips. The Johnsons had residency permits for a number of years living in Hong Kong and then New Delhi, India. Even now, at 87 years of age they spend lots of time in India.

19. Theresa Robertson, part of the Administrative team of Cornerstone Church. On Video.

20. en.wikipedia.org/wiki/John_Wayne - aka Marion Morrison. (1907–1979) was born Marion Robert Morrison at 224 South Second Street in Winterset, Iowa. Better known by his stage name John Wayne was an American film actor, director, and producer. An Academy Award winner, Wayne was among the top box office draws for three decades. The local paper, Winterset Madisonian reported on page 4 of the May 30, 1907 edition, that Wayne weighed thirteen pounds at birth. His middle name was soon changed from Robert to Mitchell when his parents decided to name their next son Robert. An enduring American icon, for several generations of Americans, he epitomized rugged masculinity and is famous for his demeanor, including his distinctive calm voice, walk, and height." Several years ago the Bishop family stopped to visit John Wayne's birthplace and took a tour of the small house. It was such fun to see it.

Chapter 9

Don't Micro-Manage How God Works

Get Rid of the War in your Spirit

The 21st century can be a time of confusion and disorder in many social circles, but it doesn't have to be. Society is re-defining itself from the youth to the aged. The young are determined to squeeze the nectar out of life, often failing to include God as much as they should; the middle aged are working feverishly to maximize their own gift to society; the older folks hoping to be remembered as having "served their generation[1] well."[2] We find the "greying factor" of church leadership is obvious. Of course it is this way, because a generation ago there were so many who responded to "the call" to serve. They are to be commended as they have carried the church to levels of success and growth unknown in previous generations. They have been responsible to establish the church, fill the seats, and lead the church; but here comes the challenge. Will the lights go out? Or will these leaders be able to graciously pass on the baton to the ones who should follow, and all this without having a spirit of war with the changes, which are sure to come?

Our first Cross-Cultural Assignment was with the Zulus

The year was 1984 and the Bishop family[3] was preparing to accept our first cross cultural ministry assignment by moving to South Africa, and the town of Amanzimtoti, to take the leadership role over a Zulu Bible College. We would be working with the Zulu[4] tribal peoples of southern Africa. We were excited about the move and the invitation by key men of God from that nation. One of those inviting us was the well known, David du Plessis, otherwise known as "Mr Pentecost."[5] One day, as we were being interviewed,

GET THE WAR OUT OF YOUR SPIRIT.

I turned to Rev. du Plessis and asked: "With this move facing us, please tell me what is the one bit of advice you'd give me to help us be successful in this mission work in South Africa?" He looked up at me and said, "Get the war out of your spirit. If there is any person, any group of people, any profession, which bothers you, then let it go." I don't know what I expected to receive from him that day, but it was not that. I thought long and hard over that one. I must admit that I have worked hard, over the years, to remove any "warring spirit" from my heart, and have been reasonably successful. I must also say that, on that day he gave me some of the most relevant counsel I have ever received. I must emulate more the Prince of Peace,[6] and I am grateful to David du Plessis for awakening in me the desire to get that area of my life in order.

I ask you, man of God, do you have any war in your spirit? As you take up the challenge to help your "successor" make a smooth transition into assuming the posture of your current assignment; will you help him? Will you work against his success? Will you step back and allow him to lead? Or will you be in competition with him? Will you be gracious in your passing of the baton? Or will he feel like you are holding onto it for an extra "split second," just to make sure he knows you're also significant? Is this a referendum about you, or is it a testimony of just how gracious you are, as a leader, in transition?

There will come a time, when age or life assignment catches up and we take a bow and step off the stage. If we do it when everyone is calling for "more, more," it will feel better than when they're saying "enough, enough." To be gracious and yield is a mark of genius and wisdom. And, on the day of your passing, all will say, "we shall miss him; what a gracious man he was."

DON'T LET THIS MOMENT BE A REFERENDUM ABOUT YOU. IT SHOULD BE A VOTE OF CONFIDENCE FOR HIM.

It is such a challenge to build for a lifetime and to be the CEO of something and then to step aside and take the second row. It is not easy, it is quiet frankly, difficult. It is a test of patience, and even feels like "second-guessing or undervaluing your own call." This call has been sacred and for so many years.[7] And yet, it is also a sad day to watch the thing you have built die, right before your eyes. To die on your watch is difficult, but to give "assistance to the dying process" is what so many have been guilty of, because they were at war with the changes, which had come inevitably.

There are countless men of God, pastors, teachers, and leaders who have done it right and passed the baton, or torch, or mantle without extreme fanfare. Yes, there was honor and respect and a blessing, which came to them, but they did it because, it was the right thing to do. They did not require unreasonable considerations, or even a gold watch.

However, and sadly, other transitions, in the end, looked more like power-grabs, or a battle of King on the Hill[8]; with anxiety and guilt on both sides of the battle lines, because of either an Absalom Spirit or a spirit of Saul,[9] being the headlines of the day.

TOSSING THOSE KEYS TO YOUR SON HAS A GOOD FEEL TO IT.

I ask: "Is there a Grandfather in the house?" Are you willing to toss the keys to your younger disciple, yielding control of the vehicle, early enough so that he does not also have grey hair? Or will you require of him to become old, set in his own ways, or impatient with you, because you made promises, which he fears you will not keep? Wisdom: Do not allow your appetite for leading to prevail when God has given you your Joshua.

Today is the first day of your future. What will you do to make sure they talk about you as a man of peace, with a gentle spirit, who required, nothing but to love and be kind? He gave what he expected in return, and loved everyone whom "God had put in his way."[10]

If this subject has spoken to you, then embrace this verse:

"He must increase, but I must decrease."[11]

Endnotes

1. Acts 13:26, speaks of how David served his generation.

2. Our fathers have mostly now gone on to be with the Lord. Tom Brokaw called them, **_"The Greatest Generation,"_** in his 1998 book by the same name. Most of those coming to age and challenged to pass the baton of leadership today, are "Baby Boomers," born after WW2, which ended on September 2, 1945.

3. Ron and Christi Bishop, and their children, Cameron (age 11) and Doryann (age 6) moved to Durban, South Africa in 1985 to assume the directorship of a Zulu Bible School in the township of Kwa Makhutha near Amanzimtoti.

4. En.wikipedia.org/wiki/Zulu_people ~ The Zulu (Zulu: amaZulu) are a Bantu ethnic group of Southern Africa and the largest ethnic group in South Africa, with an estimated 10–11 million people living mainly in the province of KwaZulu-Natal. Small numbers also live in Zimbabwe, Zambia, Tanzania and Mozambique. Their language, Zulu, is a Bantu language; more specifically, part of the Nguni subgroup.

5. Bibliography: R. P. Spittler.art. _'International Dictionary of Pentecostal and Charismatic Movements'_ 2002; David du Plessis _"A Man Called Mr. Pentecost,"_ 1977 and _'The Spirit Bade Me Go,"_ 1970.

6. Isaiah 9:6

7. In his book, **_"Lectures to My Students,"_** Charles H. Spurgeon addresses "The Call to The Ministry," and states that a man who is called into the ministry will have an "intense, all-absorbing desire for the work," the ability to do the work, and bear fruit in the work.

8. en.wikipedia.org/wiki ~ King of the Hill (game) (also known as King of the Mountain or King of the Castle) is a children's game, the object of which is to stay on top of a large hill or pile (or any other designated area) as the "King of the Hill." Other players attempt to knock the current King off the pile and take their place, thus becoming the new King of the Hill… and where winning can only be achieved at the cost of displacing the previous winner.

9. A Tale of Three Kings, by Gene Edwards. This is the story of Saul, David, and Absalom.

10. A comment by Djimon Hounsou to Heath Ledger in the movie, **_Four Feathers_**. The question was, "Why do you keep helping me?" Djimon's answer was, "God put you in my way."

11. John 3:30 KJV

Is There a Grandfather in the House?

Chapter 10

MAKE SURE YOUR SUCCESSOR HAS A TRUE NORTH

What Significance Must be Placed on Having a True North, or a Moral Compass?

Make sure your successor has a True North. Neither you, representing the past, or your successor, representing the future, will have divine approval without addressing this subject. In the life of a Christian the True North comes from obeying the Word of God.

Today I was listening to a news commentator and a politician as they discussed the value of polls in the most current debate hitting the news cycle.

The News anchor stated that a certain politician had formed her public posture based on the most recent polls. Another candidate, who was being interviewed said, "Wait a minute. What does it matter what the polls say, when we realize that this is a moral issue and polls should not drive the debate. If you have a True North, then what is right and what is wrong for humanity should drive the debate. Are we a nation, which has lost its way, so that it can only decide, which way to go based on calculating public opinion? Some questions are not answered by debate. In a civilized world, some decisions and policies should be decided based on what is right and what is wrong. We should have a conscience in these matters, and that conscience brings inner clarity. That is, unless we are no longer a civilized nation?"

Every individual, as well as nations should discover exactly what its True North, or Moral Compass is. That would settle lots of debates. If these instruments are not formed yet, or if they are ignored, then society will be like an unmanned and unanchored sailboat, adrift in "the Perfect Storm"[1]

Keep your Moral Compass Close-By, so it is Not Lost

If a society fails to enforce the values reflected in its Moral Compass, its destiny will be negatively shaped. The piranhas will rip away at the fabric of that society. The safeguard is, if there is a commitment to strong moral values enhanced by sound judgment. If the legal systems go the way of barbarism[2] in its core values, then that nation will cease to have a moral compass and will, consequently, violate their True North. It is true that you must align yourself with a magnetic field, which is consistent. If this fails to happen, and the compass points to some value system, which is detrimental to that society's well being, then self-destruction will eventually occur. If the West does not soon change

"BE ON GAURD LOOKING FOR THOSE LITTLE FOXES, WHICH THREATEN TO DESTROY ALL THAT IS OF VALUE."

SONG OF SOLOMON 2:15

its navigational coordinates, its ships are going to suffer great loss. The benefit of yielding to your True North is that when things go array you will have a nudge in your heart to bring your life back on course.

Your "True North is the internal compass that guides you successfully through life. It represents who you are as a human being at your deepest level. It is your orienting point – your fixed point in a spinning world – that helps you stay on track."[3]

The unfortunate fact seems to be that many people have dropped their compass and some hedonistic wild man has driven over it with his tractor. If a compass is in tact then it will accurately guide you to safety through uncharted territories. A compass does not change, but remains trustworthy. Being fixed to True North makes it reliable. We cannot determine, which way to go based on what's right for us, or by what gives us the greatest pleasure. There are consequences to our actions.

We are all getting more complicated. Our society, our families and our personal lives need to tighten up our grip on Christian values, and return to the basics of our True North. If we do, and if we do it soon, then we'll have the peace of repaired lives and restored relationship with God.

Endnotes

1. En.wikipedia.org/wiki/Perfect_storm - "A 'perfect storm' is an expression that describes an event where a rare combination of circumstances will aggravate a situation drastically. The term is also used to describe an actual phenomenon that happens to occur in such a confluence, resulting in an event of unusual magnitude."

2. www.merriam-webster.com/dictionary/barbarism - "Cruel and violent behavior; very rude behaviour." BING: Barbaric: "savagely cruel; exceedingly brutal"

3. *True North: Discover Your Authentic Leadership*, by Bill George with Peter Sims. The Foreword by David Gergen, Copyright © 2007 ISBN-13:978-0-7879-8751-0

Chapter 11

Decrease is the New Increase

Decrease, Increase, Humility, Growth

John the Baptist, when speaking of the Messiah, declared, "This is the assigned moment for him to move into the center, while I slip off to the sidelines."[1]

Living a motivated life can be tricky. On one hand, you get the feeling, when you look at your age, or in the mirror, or at the chapter challenge the Holy Spirit is bringing to you, that you're in "John the Baptist" mode, on the road to decrease; while on the other hand, you feel that you are at the threshold of, a new beginning. Facing a new chapter, can become exhilarating if you realize that these are the times you were built for; this very chapter; it just could be your "Esther moment."[2] Without this next chapter, your life may not be complete?

Social norms say that you should be thinking of retirement, and yet you feel that you have lots to give and lives to challenge. Of course, you are not daft; you know you cannot go on forever, and today you would agree that society is changing so fast that it is like you've taken up residence in a wind tunnel. You know that the work you have built could be even better and you're wise enough to realize that you may not be the man to take it to the next level.

Do Not be Confused with the Conflicting Attitudes of these Times

A common worldview today, in the church, is this: We must not accept decrease, because that would reflect a lack of faith, after all it is "all about me." These things come out when the flesh is speaking. It is another matter when the Holy Spirit speaks. In those times we must adhere to other types of things, namely that, which is found in the Beatitudes[3] and the Sermon on the Mount.[4] Basically, it could be said that there is a selfish vein, running through society, which refuses to accept less than the best. It can even be seen in the body language of some Christian movements.

IT COULD BE THAT DECREASE IS A PILL SOME JUST CANNOT SWALLOW, BUT IT MAY STILL BE WHAT IS NECESSARY FOR SOME OF US IN OUR ASSIGNMENT.

It has been proven that the ones who win silver, in the Olympics, compare themselves with those who won the gold, and therefore feel disappointment over having failed to win the gold. They fear that they underperformed in the events. Whereas, those who won the bronze were so excited, because they compared themselves with those who had failed to win a medal. The exhilaration is that they did well, and would not go home empty-handed.[5]

So, since you must increase, then the prevailing idea is that we must re-craft how you say things. To be politically correct, it looks like this: rule number one is to increase, never decrease. Of course John the Baptist would have had an issue with this line of thinking, but, it is the 21st century and lots of things are changing. Note: there is no rule number two, because you cannot even consider decreasing.

With that logic the New Normal is that I will increase by having the right confession so that Jesus also increases. This seems like a win-win scenario. In a world of 50 is the new 40, and we do not retire, we just re-fire; when old is the new vintage, then we must also consider that "decrease is the new increase." Now that is a tongue-tangling paragraph, but so it is with paradigms and worldviews in the 21st century. We have tweaked the principle of being real, and have elected to put up holograms and facades. At least this way, we keep our dignity and still feel good about ourselves.

Now Let's Take a Look at Another Angle to this Thought

Our best example for the thought of "He must increase, but I must decrease," is John the Baptist.[6] John's deepest destiny was activated when he recognized Jesus. He saw Jesus for who he was, the Messiah. He immediately felt overwhelmed at the fact that he was able to call out the Messiah, to introduce him to his generation. Therefore he called out, "Behold the Lamb of God, who takes away the sins of the world."[7] John the Baptist was happy to be the "voice crying in the wilderness," as prophesied by Isaiah.[8]

John did not always want to decrease, and yet, when he stood opposite the Messiah, he realized that he was mere clay, so in contrast to the Messiah, he would move to the shadows. Humility took over in his soul, as he recognized that he was made for this moment, as a prophet, and would only find his significance in reflecting the glory of Jesus. He always enjoyed baptizing as many as possible, to bring hope to his generation, but when he saw Jesus, the Holy Spirit, which was inside of him, felt a rustling.[9] It was the same thing that had caused him to leap in his mother's womb just over 30 years earlier, when Elizabeth and Mary met, both mothers being with child.[10] When John called out Jesus, even while he was baptizing Him, he had heard God speak to Jesus from heaven, saying: "You are my beloved Son, in whom I am well pleased."[11]

> JESUS LOVED JOHN THE BAPTIST, BUT STILL HAD TO CAUTION HIM SAYING: "BLESSED IS HE WHO IS NOT OFFENDED IN ME."

There did, however, come a time when John allowed his circumstances to undermine his judgment. John had served as a prophetic voice in the land and accused King Herod of adultery with his brother's wife, Herodias. In retaliation Herod had imprisoned him.[12] Finally, even John the Baptist became discouraged with what was going on in his own life. He began to second-guess his own revelation and sent two of his disciples to Jesus asking: "Are you the Messiah we've been expecting, or should we keep looking for someone else?"[13] Jesus did not stop to answer their question, but continued in plain view working miracles and teaching, over the next few hours. Then, finally, He turned to the disciples of John and said: "Go your way, and tell John what things ye have seen and heard; how that the blind see, the lame walk, the lepers are cleansed, the deaf hear, the dead are raised, and to the poor the gospel is preached." Jesus concluded by saying, "And blessed is he, whosoever shall not be offended in me." It is clear that Jesus was sending a message to John, letting him know that he realized that John, just may be a bit offended at him, mainly because his own personal fate was at risk.[14]

Yes, the Lord wants us to abound, to prosper, to succeed, and to be blessed. Yes, He wants you to be strong, healed, whole, and able to abound in this life. He would rather you experience wealth than poverty, to be victorious and never defeated. He wants you to accomplish your dream, fulfill your destiny, and experience abundance. There is the promise that whatever you sacrifice and give up shall be returned to you "pressed down, shaken together and running over."[15] You can trust that when you need a word in your mouth the Holy Spirit will be faithful in that same hour to fill your mouth[16] and then to protect you when your enemy comes in against you, by mounting up like a flood[17] against Satan to defeat every one of his efforts to destroy you.

Take a look at the fact that, not only did God call Elisha to overwhelm the enemy with the power of God, in miraculous ways, but he also called men like Jeremiah, Hosea and even Job to show the world a different side of God and how He works in the affairs of men. God wants to redeem all of mankind, but must work in different ways, based on where they are in their own life's journey. We see clearly that in the lives of the people of this world, the pendulum is swinging from one extreme to the other. We, the children of God, are their best examples, as they watch our lives, and how God is for us, and with us. It is a fact that some just will not get the memo if God does not use his vessels of honor, to showcase His care. It is not pleasant for you, when God calls you right into the midst of catastrophic situations and calamitous struggles, but His grace will be sufficient to help you, nevertheless.[18] Sometimes, what the world needs, with all of its bad choices and disastrous consequences, is to see that we can have an inner peace, even when bad things happen to good people. That level of showcasing God's handiwork must not be lost to those who watch us. It is with this heart of hearts that Paul spoke on this matter.[19]

You, and you alone can truly grasp the nature of the destiny of God in your life. I do not know who will read these words. It may be someone in a part of the world, who may never really suffer persecution, and therefore will live out his or her days in peace. Or it could be someone in a part of the world who comes face to face with persecution and evil on a regular basis. So, this is not a "one size fits all" word. You must ask what God will require of you, and then decide if you are one of those who will truly increase or decrease. Whoever you are, you must decrease, when coming face to face with Almighty God, the Creator and Master Potter, because, you really are a piece of clay. It is not about you, and it will never be about you, but always about Him.[20]

The Bud Biffle Story

Silas K. (Bud) Biffle[21] was a dear friend. Bud was an excellent example for so many of us on so many levels. He was born in Kennett, MO and grew up son of a pastor in Joplin, MO, an army veteran of WW2, and a graduate of Central Bible College in Springfield, MO. He served as a pastor first in Branson, Missouri, and then in both Nebraska and Ohio. Later on in life, Bud founded the National Investment Finance Services, a company that helped finance-building programs for churches and other institutions throughout the USA. He served churches and fellowships as treasurer and was always available for a good dose of wisdom, whenever any of us were in need of it.

For the last several years of his life, he served in a voluntary capacity for a large fellowship of churches in Irving, Texas. He was not so concerned for titles, as much as he saw things in light of the opportunity to serve. I admired this man and sincerely appreciated his insight, when I found myself in need of good solid counsel. He certainly was a blessing to me when I needed just one more voice to hear from as I faced a major decision. Full of humor, and all seasoned by a deep fatherly voice, I often thought of him as the man to pattern after, as a grandfather.

The fact that I met him in his latter years has left me with an appreciation of his interest in giving of his time and gifts to something he believed in. He gave and gave when he could have continued his career. He was more interested in being of service to something as valuable as helping others and just being a part of a bigger vision. He never required the spotlight to focus on him, but was a giver in every area of his life. When Bud Biffle passed away, so many of us have missed him and celebrated the Moral Compass and True North that so clearly defined him.

Although Bud Biffle was an accountant, had served as the president of a financial corporation, and was Senior Pastor of three churches, he did not feel it was beneath him to volunteer for "The Fellowship"[22] in Irving, Texas, even into his late 80s. He volunteered to answer the phones, work with the leaders on the finances, and help in anyway they wished. He was truly a pleasant grandfather, and we all loved him.

Endnotes

1. John 3:30 MSG. Jesus must take "center stage," while I slip off the stage and to the sidelines. History has declared loudly that, "It is not about me." In the NLT it says it this way, "He must become greater and greater, and I must become less and less."

2. Esther 4:14 AMP "For if you keep silent at this time, relief and deliverance shall arise for the Jews from elsewhere, but you and your father's house will perish. And who knows but that you have come to the kingdom for such a time as this and for this very occasion?" An "Esther moment" refers to the climactic moment or purpose for a life.

3. Matthew 5:1-12 The Beatitudes, as Jesus begins to give the "Sermon on the Mount."

4. Matthew 5-7 The sermon on the mount, by Jesus

5. www.bbc.com/future/story/20120810-olympic-lessons-in-regret - ***Why Winning a Bronze Metal beats a Silver.*** The Olympian who wins Silver feels slighted that they failed to win the Gold. The one who wins the Bronze, however, is just so happy to have won this much, and did not go home empty handed. So, in photos of the actual ceremony, the Silver winner looks unhappy and the Bronze winner is ecstatic.

6. John 3:30 MSG. Jesus must take "center stage," while I slip off the stage and to the sidelines. History has declared loudly that, "It is not about me." In the NLT it says it this way, "He must become greater and greater, and I must become less and less."

7. John 1:26-31 NLT "John told them, 'I baptize with water, but right here in the crowd is someone you do not recognize. Though his ministry follows mine, I'm not even worthy to be his slave and untie the straps of his sandal.' This encounter took place in Bethany, an area east of the Jordan River, where John was baptizing. The next day John saw Jesus coming toward him and said, "Look! The Lamb of God who takes away the sin of the world! He is the one I was talking about when I said, 'A man is coming after me who is far greater than I am, for he existed long before me.' I did not recognize him as the Messiah, but I have been baptizing with water so that he might be revealed to Israel."

8. Isaiah 40 NKJV "Comfort, yes, comfort my people!" Says your God. "Speak comfort to Jerusalem, and cry out to her, that her warfare is ended, that her iniquity is pardoned; for she has received from the Lord's hand double for all her sins. The voice of one crying in the wilderness: Prepare the way of the Lord;make straight in the desert a highway for our God."

9. Dictionary.reference.com/browse/rustle - Rustled - A verb. To rustle, as in John's case, was to experience an inner movement in the very soul. It could be explained as simply as this: "To make a succession of slight sounds, as of parts rubbing gently one on another, as leaves, silks, or papers."

10. Luke 1:41 NLT "At the sound of Mary's greeting, Elizabeth's child leaped within her, and Elizabeth was filled with the Holy Spirit."

11. Mark 1:11 NKJV

12. John 14:3 NLT "For Herod had arrested and imprisoned John as a favor to his wife Herodias (the former wife of Herod's brother Philip)."

13. Luke 7:20 NLT John's two disciples found Jesus and said to him, "John the Baptist sent us to ask, 'Are you the Messiah we've been expecting, or should we keep looking for someone else?'"

14. Luke 7:21-23

15. Luke 6:38 NLT "Give, and you will receive. Your gift will return to you in full—pressed down, shaken together to make room for more, running over, and poured into your lap. The amount you give will determine the amount you get back."

16. Matthew 10:19 MSG "Don't be naive. Some people will impugn your motives; others will smear your reputation—just because you believe in me. Don't be upset when they haul you before the civil authorities. Without knowing it, they've done you—and me—a favor, given you a platform for preaching the kingdom news! And don't worry about what you'll say or how you'll say it. The right words will be there; the Spirit of your Father will supply the words."

17. Isaiah 59:19 MSG In the Dutch Bible it states that, "When the enemy comes in to destroy you, then the Lord will rise up like a flood against him." This is because the translators understood the comma to be in a different place and that, I found to be amazing. Then in the Message Bible, it states in Isaiah 59:19: "In the west they'll fear the name of God, in the east they'll fear the glory of God, For he'll arrive like a river in flood stage, whipped to a torrent by the wind of God."

18. 2 Corinthians 12:9 KJV "And he hath said unto me, my grace is sufficient for thee: for my power is made perfect in weakness. Most gladly therefore will I rather glory in my weaknesses, that the power of Christ may rest upon me."

19. In Romans, 9:1-4 Paul addresses his commitment and willingness to be a vessel of use for eternal purpose for those he cares about. In this case, it was the people of Israel. For us it may be another group who are dear to our hearts. Here are Paul's words: Romans 9:1-4 NLT "With Christ as my witness, I speak with utter truthfulness. My conscience and the Holy Spirit confirm it. My heart is filled with bitter sorrow and unending grief for my people, my Jewish brothers and sisters. I would be willing to be forever cursed — cut off from Christ! — if that would save them. They are the people of Israel, chosen to be God's adopted children. God revealed his glory to them. He made covenants with them and gave them his law. He gave them the privilege of worshiping him and receiving his wonderful promises.

20. If you can please, take a few minutes to read from the writings of the Apostle John. Read the first chapters of the Gospel of John and the book of Revelation. These confirm the high and holy value of Jesus in the place He occupies now.

21. Silas K. (Bud) Biffle. Passed away at age 86, on March 25, 2012. At the passing of this great man, he was volunteering his financial perspective to the services of the Full Gospel Fellowship of Churches and Ministers International.

22. www.thefellowshiptoday.com - The Full Gospel Fellowship of Churches and Ministers International, commonly referred to simply as "The Fellowship."

Chapter 12

So, You Wish to Die with Your Boots on?

Undefeated, Unyielding, Untrusting

Let Us Now Turn the Spotlight Back to You

You are well aware that you have a son in the gospel. He is primed, full of wisdom, and with the right heart to take it all forward and to complete the vision. He will do things differently, but you did things differently, than your fathers in the Lord; so what's the problem?

Often I am riding with a friend in a third-world nation and find the danger really concerns me. His driving style is so different than mine. He clearly has a different view of the road and the challenges before him. His reaction times are different and his responses are more abrupt. I look over at the driver and think, "he has been driving a very long time and is still alive. We will likely make it to our destination." So I then close my eyes for a few minutes, as a means of self-discipline. This way I am able to consider that although I am not driving, I will survive. I decide to let the young man drive. So my suggestion to you is, "close your eyes, pastor, and let it go."

The big question keeps coming up, as you ask yourself: "Are you willing to take a step up, so that you become a grandfather, rather than just a father? Your thoughts go to: "I've been a father for several years and that has been fun; but how good it sounds to actually admit to myself, 'I am a grandfather.'" The challenge is that you have to release yourself to this new chapter, rather than fight it, or oppose the transition. Guard against being in denial about your life chapter, and embrace all the options you are able to enjoy.

Only Leaders can Produce Leaders

Now lets talk about the differences in store for you when you move from filling a "father's shoes" to stepping up and into the roll of being a "grandfather." You say, "That sounds so old." Let's face it; God has new and delightful doors to open up to you if you will embrace who you have become. The reality is that, if you do not move forward and upward, then you just may be the one who jeopardizes your own legacy. What is your responsibility, as the set man?[1] You are to multiply leaders, inspire new life and vision, and all this realizing that only leaders can produce leaders.

ONLY LEADERS CAN PRODUCE LEADERS.

If you are to affirm your sons, then it can be done better as a grandfather, which is a non-threatening roll. It is time to step up from being a father, become a grandfather, and let a new life for you and your son in the gospel begin. This way he will achieve his own assignment. At that point you must step back, far back, and let him take the lead.

The Apostle Paul wrote, "You have heard me teach things that have been confirmed by reliable witnesses. Now teach these truths to other trustworthy people who will be able to pass them on to others."[2] Notice that Paul is referring to four different generations:

* Paul (the one writing)

* Timothy (Paul's son in the Gospel)

* Timothy's disciples (Faithful Men)

* Others

If you recall your own mentor, then it is possible to see five generations or levels impacted from your own ministry.

I hope you have been thinking along these lines. I trust you have realized your need to have a "Timothy"[3] and that you have accepted the one God brought to you.

The challenge is simply this: If you do not become a loving grandfather, then after you pass the baton,[4] or the torch, or the mantle to your successor; you must uproot your household, and move far away, or you will be considered a threat to the stability of the work. Get proficient at tossing the keys to your son in the gospel. Let him drive, and you just take in the view. If you allow the grace you have talked about to take a greater place in your life, then you just may be able to continue residing in your city, be with your family, and remain a part of the congregation. But if you are "testy" then your days are numbered.

Some say, "I Plan to Die with My Boots On."

I have overheard more than one grandfather make boastful statements, which revealed the commitment to their original call. It may not make sense to other generations, but it certainly reflects an ironclad commitment to that call. Some of those statements are:

* "I have never found the word 'retire' in the Bible. I do not intend to ever retire."

* "My desire is to die while I'm standing behind the pulpit."

* "I plan to die with my boots on."

My first thought, was a question: just how much do you want to leave your church traumatized and wounded? This could leave those who remain, with traumatic counseling sessions afterwards. To be honest I actually knew of two churches where this happened, and I would not describe the aftermath as pleasant, joyful, or complimentary. But last week I heard of a third church where this took place. I don't think anyone present in those services were overjoyed that a man of God died while they were sitting in the service. I think a lot of wailing was more the order of the day, on those days. There were no compliments being hurled at the pulpit, but rather, "I wish he had not died with me in the congregation that day, and I'm not sure how long it will be before I don't think of it so much."

"YOU WILL KNOW I AM RETIRING WHEN YOU SEE MY CASKET LEAVING THE BUILDING."

Another trivia question may be added to our list: "Where were you when the pastor fell out in the pulpit and died?"

At the end of the day, the question remains, "Do you feel this way because you're concerned about your legacy?" Remember that there is life after a lifetime of ministry. If you have been a good leader, relax and don't take, even your ministry so seriously that you would go out feet first, unless it is as a martyr. Step up, become a grandfather and mentor, or coach someone from a position of strength. You can make a statement that you want to die with your boots on, if you wish. But, if you do, could it reflect that you have no trust in the next generation and its ability to take the church to the next level. It also states that you feel that you are the epitome of "all wisdom" and have taken the church as high as it is possible for it to go. Just remember this: many things will change as soon as you do pass from this life.

PILGRIM, JUST CALL ME THE DUKE, OR JOHN WAYNE, IF YOU LIKE.

Keep this in mind: If your death is in public view, there will be an emergency meeting of your leaders to make lots of changes to protect themselves in the future. They might even seem a little gun-shy, when it comes to the surprise factor of witnessing such a traumatic event. Leaders want to protect the wellbeing of their families, and this is too shocking. It may even leave a black cloud hanging over the church, in the minds of those who had been considering visiting your particular church. It may even seem a bit like the concern over buying a house where someone has just died in the kitchen.

Now, if you are a reasonably young man, and you die prematurely taking everyone by surprise, then that may be another matter. But if you have lived out your days, then those of us, who remain, will be praying for the church to survive after your death.

There Should Never be Competition with the Son

The body language of grandfathers is to stand back and enjoy enabling their sons to become the fathers. Grandfathers insist that their sons take the lead.

One of the most difficult observations is when men, who are really grandfathers, compete with their sons for the prestige, the titles, the money, and the limelight. If they feel that no one can do it like they can, then their older years will be cold and lonely. One principle to keep in mind is this one: "Sons do grow up," and we realize that eventually we all shall pass from this life.

LETS PICK OUT A TABLE AND ARM WRESTLE, I CAN STILL WIN THIS ONE! LET ME FIRST PUT DOWN MY CANE.

Many fathers have lived full lives, and now enjoy great respect as loved and cherished leaders, but sadly do not know how to spend their "grandfather currency."

As I get older I have less living mentors; but the valuable lessons they taught me will always be with me. The few living mentors I have left are great-grandfathers now. They cannot boast of being "fathers," or even grandfathers, but must own up to being great grandfathers.

Now That is Enough About You. Let's Talk About Your Son.

Tell us about your son in the gospel. Is he married? Is he a father yet? How old are his children? Please do not tell me that you have kept him in the roll of "son," and he is about to become a grandfather.

What is wrong with this picture? If your son is soon to be a grandfather, then what does that make you? … Great-grandfather!

Would you agree with me now that being a grandfather doesn't sound so bad?

Sometimes Our Body Language Reveals What is in Our Thoughts. Perhaps You can Relate to One of These:

* I cannot imagine that God would consider requiring decrease of me. My theology just does not allow this.

* I must increase so He can increase. "It really is all about me."

* To even speak of decrease shows a lack of faith.

* I'm afraid that, if I confess decrease then it might happen.

* Paul, Jesus, and John the Baptist were politically incorrect and therefore would not understand our challenges today.

Here is Something to Consider

The mindset, or worldview of this generation may be out of alignment with the way God thinks. When John the Baptist faced off with Jesus on the banks of the Jordan River, he was engulfed in humility and submitted himself, his life goals, and his ministry to the will and purposes of his creator. Is it possible that some 21st century leaders are so corrupted and sabotaged by an environment of "carnal flesh,"[5] that they have been blinded and cannot see the bigger picture?

Tempering this generation is the greed for personal advancement and the climate of political correctness. It should occur to us that we are "clay" and He is the Potter? Clay must yield, when confronted by the Potter. If you wish to become cutting edge, in time for eternity, then consider that decrease may feel good, as it also relieves you of burdensome responsibilities, and gives you breathing space to enjoy the new chapter you are in?

I ask you again, could it be that: Decrease is the new Increase?

Endnotes

1. Blog.frankdamazio.com/2011/07/the-set-man ~ The Set man ~ ***"Effective Keys to Successful Leadership."*** The senior (or lead) pastor is the key leader in God's leadership structure. Helmsman. The set man stands as a helmsman in his leadership position to direct and manage the church in all areas of spiritual life and vision. He steers the ship according to his God-given gift to lead, his biblical knowledge of the God-given vision, and his proven character. The spiritual advancement of the church depends on spiritual leaders who are capable of breaking through obstacles at hand. The set man is key to moving the people of God forward.

2. 2 Timothy 2:2 NLT

3. Your son in the Gospel, or your successor, can be described as your "Timothy," or your "Joshua."

4. idioms.thefreedictionary.com "Pass the torch." "This metaphoric expression alludes to the ancient Greek torch race, in which a lighted torch was passed from one runner to the next." The idea is the same as "Pass the baton," or as in the case of an ancient Biblical prophet, such as Elijah, who passes the mantle to his successor, Elisha.

5. We are made up of both "flesh" and "spirit." The part of mankind which aligns better with the things of God is that spiritual side of our lives, whereas the flesh side of us often lends itself to carnality.

Is There a Grandfather in the House?

Chapter 13

BE GRACIOUS, A LOT DEPENDS ON IT!

GOOD MANNERS AND GRACIOUSNESS ARE NOT THE SAME.

Graciousness is an aura. It is something that you are, even when taken by surprise, caught off guard, put in a difficult situation or challenged by insistent people. It is natural to be kind to good people and accommodating to those who do not expect so much of you. But when you are on a time schedule, or feel threatened, or are in your compartment of creativity, then you have to be especially on your toes to make sure that you remain civil and gracious. Those are the times when you can quickly and easily fall off the wagon. Life is a test.

How would you describe your tongue? Does your tongue go off on people when you feel threatened? Are you quite masterful when you are put in a corner, saying just the right word to correct; are you testy and able to put them in their place and discipline someone who has approached you without permission? These are not the characteristics of the gracious.

People around you likely need friends, they need fathers, and

LOOSE CANNONS CAN GO OFF WHEN LEAST EXPECTED. they need comfort. Many of those near you are filled with fears of all kinds and often for good reason. Do not become one of those who plant seeds of doubt, fear, frustration and hesitation in their hearts. Work on being approachable and do not allow a corridor of defense to be lifted up around you.

You Must Not Have a Perimeter Alarm Around You

I have met pastors, and leaders in many different fields who have perimeter alarms, or invisible fences, which kept them at arm's length. My feeling was that people like me just could not get close, or the loud bells would go off, security guards would descend on ropes from black helicopters and I would be instantly vaporized if I came closer. I may have, even upon invitation gotten reasonably close to them, but I never felt comfortable or welcomed. These kinds of leaders may build followings, but they are likely very lonely, because of their fears of being used and too available. I just never saw, in them that element of graciousness. I was of the impression that they were too distant and closed off from the little people. Some of them even appeared to be elitists.

I read Ken Blanchard's book about S. Truett Cathy called, "The Generosity Factor" and was impressed that Cathy was, not only a Godly man, but also a gracious man. With his open door policy and his kind and generous nature, I felt he was a man I'd rather emulate.[1]

"Always keep your words soft and sweet, just in case you have to eat them."[2] It is important to grow old graciously and to pass the baton successfully. Don't be a grumpy old man.[3] Keep your character in check, and protect your image as much as possible. Don't lose your personality crediting it to having a bad day, or because of your medication. I have had some friends whom I had to forgive, because, later I'd learn that they were probably having a bad medication day. They were testy, unforgiving, ungracious and overly difficult. Pass the test every day. Today is the best time to begin making sure of that.

Humanity is weak. Of course there is the athlete and there is the odd one who accomplishes so much and with such fantastic style that we all salute and cast our crowns at their feet, in a sense. And yet, bad days, unclimbable mountains and insurmountable circumstances can bring, even the best, to their knees and disable an individual in challenging ways.

GRANDFATHERS ARE NEVER GROUCHY, SELF-CENTERED OR IN A BAD MOOD. UNLESS YOU ARE THE EXCEPTION.

It is only by the grace and favor of God that we can abound. The will within us can draw us out, or drive us onward to achieve what few men or women can accomplish. For these things we must give honor and commendations. It is a fact that there are levels of leadership that can best be described as "captains of tens," captains of hundreds" and "captains of thousands."[4] Then above that are majors, colonials and generals. As we stand facing these men we must give honor, where "honor is due."[5]

Not everyone is gracious. Many people have good manners and are polite, but to be gracious is another matter. I would go so far as to say that not every minister of the Gospel, or every older leader is gracious. It would do you good to sit down and make a list of those whom you consider the most gracious people you know. The lack of length in your list will surprise you. There are many who are friendly, and generous, and outgoing, but graciousness is another issue worth pursuing in your own life.[6]

I am in the process of making my list of gracious men I know. My list is getting long, as I am blessed with lots of friends, but it could, it should, be longer. Lord help all of my friends to strive for graciousness.

Endnotes

1. This book is a must read: The Generosity Factor, By Ken Blanchard on the life, accomplishments, gracious nature and wisdom of S. Truett Cathy. Cathy was founder of Chick-fil-A and passed away in 2014 at age 93.

2. www.goodreads.com/quotes/759981 - "Always keep your words soft and sweet, just in case you have to eat them" – Andy Rooney

3. www.nbcnews.com/id/50305818/ns/health-mens_health/t/get-my-lawn-why-some-older-men-get-so-grouchy - Grumpiness is often related to a fall in the levels of Testosterone. If you come to that stage in life, it may be advisable to have this tested. There just may be help on the way.

4. Deuteronomy 1:15 KJV "So I took the chief of your tribes, wise men, and known, and made them heads over you, captains over thousands, and captains over hundreds, and captains over fifties, and captains over tens, and officers among your tribes."

5. Romans 13:7 AMP "Render to all men their dues. (Pay) taxes to whom taxes are due, respect to whom respect is due and honor to whom honor is due."

6. www.esquire.com/news-politics/a22372/how-to-be-gracious-0513 - "How to be Gracious and Why" - Graciousness looks easy, but of course, it is not. Do not mistake mere manners for graciousness. Manners are rules. Helpful, yes. But graciousness reflects a state of being; it emanates from your inventory of self. Start with what you already possess... When wandering the world, forget your business cards. Don't look for more contacts. Instead, observe. Say hello to the people you see every day, but don't make a fetish out of it. Stay interested in others. Be generous in your attentions but not showy. Don't wink, snap your fingers, high-five, or shout; but do laugh with those who do. It bears repeating: Look around. Remember names. Remember where people were born.

Is There a Grandfather in the House?

Chapter 14

EMBRACE THE PROCESS

ENJOY THE VINTAGE—GOD SAW THIS COMING IN ADVANCE

Life is a process, and aging is not the enemy; embrace it as a friend. Wisdom comes with the years, which have been tempered by experience and the Holy Spirit.

May I ask you, "What vintage are you? If you were wine, how would you taste?" Aging is not all bad, but hides within its secret compartments many positive discoveries. Have you ever thought of how beneficial the aging process is in your life? Would you see yourself as a "better you," in your younger times, or a "better you," after the years have passed? How have you responded to all the pressures, tensions, challenges, successes and failures, which have come your way?

Let me give you a practical example. The aging process is a precious part of the maturing of traditional Balsamic vinegar, vintage wines and the lives of seasoned leaders.

The Aging of Balsamic Vinegar in Modena, Italy

Traditional Balsamic Vinegar is made in only one place on earth, the Italian provinces of Reggio Emilia and neighboring Modena. It comes from the juice of grape pressings. "The aging process is a serious undertaking that can take 12-100 years, and requires meticulous care. As the syrup thickens and evaporates, it is moved into successively smaller barrels, made of different woods, such as cherry, chestnut and ash."[1] Traditional Balsamic Vinegar is, required by the European Union to bear the D.O.P.[2] stamp of certification. It is subjected to strict aging restrictions. Therefore, they set the standards for bringing this product to the market. This increases the value and insures the quality and consistency. It is well worth all the effort, because all Balsamic Vinegar is not equal. Some is worth $100 or more for 100ml (3 oz.), while others are worth only $5.99 for the same volume. Of course there is an industrialized method for producing balsamic vinegar. This method does cut quality, flavor and even desired usage; consequently bringing the price down to prices anyone can afford. This makes the product available to everyone, but only the traditional Balsamic Vinegar is true to the quality enjoyed during medieval times.

TRADITIONAL BALSAMIC VINEGAR AGES 12-100 YEARS AND COSTS UP TO $100 FOR 3 OUNCES.

While visiting Modena, Italy with a friend,[3] who pastored nearby, we were educated, in a casual conversation with a restaurant owner, on the history and very nature of Balsamic Vinegar. I was amazed to hear of how similar the process is to making wine, and yet wine it is not. The value of the aging process is significant and the result of engaging in its making is worthwhile.

When we look at the aging processes of our lives we discover that time can also do good things in us. At the same time it is contingent on how you respond to the conditions and circumstances that surround you. It is a wonderful thing to see those who age well, and have the gift of being able to take all of the negatives of life, turn them around and transform them into positives. They easily turn their lemons into lemonade. They have learned to adapt to anything life has brought their way. The question still remains: do you pass the test each day, or do you live in reaction mode? If you are always on guard then you will likely be frustrated, overly cautious, if not slightly paranoid. The secret is to pray a lot, forgive often and learn to trust that God will hold your life in the palm of His hand. This results in a peaceful nature and a mature outlook on life.

LEADERS GO THROUGH AN AGING PROCESS THAT CREATES BOLD FLAVORS AND AROMAS.

In contrast, some are challenged with being toxic agers. Time, and their failure to proactively respond to the challenges they have faced can become their enemy. These folks can actually produce a noxious air, which can best be compared with the wrong end of a magnet. Instead of people being drawn to them, they are last seen disappearing over the horizon, as they run with their hands in the air, screaming "let me get out of Dodge."[4] Toxic aging is often as a result of gunnysacking[5] unresolved issues throughout the life of the individual. Another way to describe this is when the "old demons" visit, even at the Convalescent Home.

It is a good thing to become "vintage"… to accumulate years, to become seasoned and wise, as a sage. The years can potentially add to you flavor, a certain robustness, boldness, confidence, humility and sweetness. Otherwise, we can appear, to those around us as boring, out of date, self-centered, self-righteous and short sighted.

109

Growing and developing is a normal part of life. Stay focused on daily growth by reading, praying, observing others, and listening. It is great to engage in conversations on current events, sports, politics, and the stock market; and yet, it is imperative that you raise the bar of influence and mentor your friends and colleagues on things above and not just earthly. One of the ways I have responded to this is by asking, at the end of many conversations, "How can I pray with you? What can I pray with you about?" This usually injects a mood into the atmosphere, which takes us to a new reality. Throughout the years, even with non-Christians, I have discovered that the mood in the room changes, instantly and they come back with a problem, or a dilemma, which has been plaguing them. Try it sometime and see if it will help you to speak more effectively into a life.

Take the long view![6] Ask yourself this question: "In whatever remaining time I have on this earth, what can I do to fine-tune my own life? How can I improve?" Sit with someone you trust and ask them to help you see your nature as clearly as possible. Let me give you a hint, the Holy Spirit, assuming you have allowed Him to live deep inside of you, probably has already been whispering to you about attitude. Have you been listening? Would you obey, if He did speak to you in the night? I keep a note pad near my bed. Whenever the Holy Spirit awakens me, or speaks to me in a dream, then I take a few moments to jot down the simplest of references to remind me tomorrow morning. If I am working through a challenge, often I will awaken during the night to just the right solution, or perhaps a caution on my normal approach to it. That is when that note pad also comes in handy. Now if you are really not interested in self-improvement, then say hello to "toxic aging." You grow by taking a long view at life. See how this will affect, not just the present, but also the future.

Endnotes

1. www.huffingtonpost.com/2014/06/09 written by: Julie R. Thomson

2. www.modenafinefoods.com ~ The certification "DOP" – Denomination of Protected Origin, is given by the European Union and identifies the name of a product whose production, processing, and preparation must take place in a specific geographical area and characterized by a recognized know-how.

3. Our friends are Mario & Sheila Scorziello, Christian workers for many years in Italy.

4. Wiktionary.org ~ Dodge City, Kansas was a busy cattle town in the late 19th century and the site of a famous set of gun battles called the Dodge City War. In this case the suggestion is to leave, in particular to leave a difficult or dangerous environment with all possible haste.

5. Wikipedia.org ~ Gunnysacking has been described as 'an alienating fight tactic in which a person saves up, or gunnysacks, grievances until the sack gets too heavy and bursts, and old hostilities pour out'. (A Gunny Sack is a cloth container used for carrying or storing things).

6. ***Perspective: Devotional thoughts for men.*** By Richard C. Halverson, Copyright 1976

Is There a Grandfather in the House?

Chapter 15

Don't Try to be Something you're Not

Real, Genuine, No Regrets

Real[1] is a good word. It separates itself from all things, which are illusions and bogus. There are many real leaders, real and caring friends, and there are so many who represent the genuine. No one likes a fake. You would certainly prefer the real deal rather than a counterfeit. Fake smiles, disingenuous personalities and feigned[2] interest are characteristics, which lack quality. Don't try to be something you're not; but use all you have to represent those things that are good.

If you are a leader, and plan to leave your best mark on society, then this is something you must consider, when you determine to become "Real."

Take this from Margery Williams:

"'REAL ISN'T HOW YOU ARE MADE,' SAID THE SKIN HORSE. 'IT'S A THING THAT HAPPENS TO YOU. WHEN A CHILD LOVES YOU FOR A LONG, LONG TIME, NOT JUST TO PLAY WITH, BUT REALLY LOVES YOU, THEN YOU BECOME REAL.'

'DOES IT HURT?' ASKED THE RABBIT.

'SOMETIMES,' SAID THE SKIN HORSE, FOR HE WAS ALWAYS TRUTHFUL. 'WHEN YOU ARE REAL YOU DON'T MIND BEING HURT.'

'DOES IT HAPPEN ALL AT ONCE, LIKE BEING WOUND UP,' HE ASKED, 'OR BIT BY BIT?'

'IT DOESN'T HAPPEN ALL AT ONCE,' SAID THE SKIN HORSE. 'YOU BECOME. IT TAKES A LONG TIME. THAT'S WHY IT DOESN'T HAPPEN OFTEN TO PEOPLE WHO BREAK EASILY, OR HAVE SHARP EDGES, OR WHO HAVE TO BE CAREFULLY KEPT. GENERALLY, BY THE TIME YOU ARE REAL, MOST OF YOUR HAIR HAS BEEN LOVED OFF, AND YOUR EYES DROP OUT AND YOU GET LOOSE IN THE JOINTS AND VERY SHABBY. BUT THESE THINGS DON'T MATTER AT ALL, BECAUSE ONCE YOU ARE REAL YOU CAN'T BE UGLY, EXCEPT TO PEOPLE WHO DON'T UNDERSTAND.'" [3]

To be real is to be genuine, authentic, bona fide and leaving no room for the phony or artificial. Genuine things are true or authentic. When you talk about people, being genuine it has to do with being sincere. I was having lunch with a pastor several years ago for the first time, having just met him. I knew he was well connected with lots of churches and pastors, but was taken aback when, over the course of a one-hour luncheon, he referred three times to his "1,500 dollar suit," and all this as he flipped open his coat so that I could almost see the label. I was underwhelmed, to say the least.

WHEN YOU LOOK INTO THE MIRROR, DO YOU EVER SEE THE SKIN HORSE?

In June of 1984, I heard an old friend of mine, Judson Cornwall[4] refer to his suit in a conference in Blountville, Tennessee, by saying, "I buy my suits from a famous French designer known as Jacques C Penné." He was actually mocking such things as boasting about how much your "things" cost. Judson was making reference to the JC Penny Store.[5]

Who are you? Do you really know who you are?

Don't covet someone else's abilities, looks, talents, education, or advantages, but look introspectively to determine your own assets. You must not squander your opportunity by living a one-talent life when you have ten talents.[6] Have you ever calculated how many talents you were given? I have often thought about it, but likely will not know until eternity what talents I actually received from my creator. Still, I do believe that you can know, by instinct, what your gifts are and then begin doing what you can about placing value on them. It is like faith. You were given a measure of faith,[7] and must activate that faith, so that your life is full of vision, purpose and fulfilment. Your talents just may be a manifestation of your gifts, and being real reflects your motives and intensity of purpose.

A WELL BALANCED LIFE HAS AS MANY DIMENSIONS AS A RUBIK'S CUBE.

Be willing to explore your other talents. You have a variety of characteristics in your nature, as well as interests that you have never tapped into. How many of your dimensions have you enjoyed, and how many talents have you put to full use? So many live their lives as one-talent people. As in the case of the Rubik's Cube[8], you should attempt to discover more dimensions to your true identity and what makes you tick.

The Potter's House is Good for the Soul

My landlord, while we lived in Germany's Black Forest,[9] was a world-class potter renowned in his work with Japanese style pottery. I used to sit with him in his workshop, watching him form the soft clay. The vessels he created were both beautiful and expensive. Herr Kersten would turn the clay on his foot pedal style wheel to form the vessel he wanted. Sometimes the vessel was large and ornate and sometimes small and practical. His fingers were quite sensitive, as the wet clay turned at his fingertips. He was also aggressive in removing any stones he discovered.

DON'T BE DRY CLAY ON THE POTTER'S WHEEL.

If he detected that the stone was too embedded in the clay of the vessel, he would dig his finger into the clay, removing the stone; then he would stop the wheel and press with his hands downward to flatten the clay, so that he could begin again. At this early stage of the process, nothing was sacred. A rock embedded in the side of a forming lump of clay could be easily removed. If this artist had been hesitant then more time and energy would be invested. Without a second thought he would right the wrong, and make the correction.

After working for the longest time on a vase, or vessel of some type, he would set it aside and allow it to harden by drying. He was ever vigilant to discover flaws, but working carefully to minimize the chance of a bad investment.

Our family observed, as the Kersten family would bring in large stacks of wood for use in the elongated, igloo shaped kiln[10], which he had built with his own hands. The day for firing up the huge cave kiln was approaching. One night, we came in to see the Kersten's camping out at the kiln, frequently peering through the five inch hole to observe the pottery, which had been arranged in a progressive step fashion within. This very hot process went on uninterrupted, for three days and nights. Sometimes, even after midnight, I'd go out to sit with a member of his family, while they engaged in this shift work. I never knew who would be out there, but would sit and drink hot

WHEN WE GET INTO THE KILN OF THE POTTER, WE LOOSE OUR COLORS AND BECOME TRANSLUCENT.

chocolate in the cool night, with the family member to keep them company. Occasionally, I'd look into the small hole to see the vessels, which would later be brown, or grey or earth tones, but were now translucent and nearly white. The temperature had risen to as much as 1400°C (2,500 °F). As I stood there it reminded me of the "fiery furnace" Nebuchadnezzar had built to make sure no one failed to worship his golden image.[11]

Finally, after three full days of firing the cave kiln, we awakened to see that all was quiet with no one at the site with all the family asleep. Several more hours would pass for cooling, before they'd break open the brick kiln and start their evaluation. I was intrigued to see them holding each piece up to the light of the sun. Then they'd occasionally bash a vessel mercilessly onto a huge rock in the garden. They explained that they had no place for a flawed vessel, and must destroy it, as they refused to take a chance of a flawed vessel being sold as his handiwork.

This has left me with the sense of awareness to insure that, if there is anything in me that is other than "real," then it must be purged from my heart and removed, so that there'll be no cracks in my vessel, no flaws in my integrity, or blemishes in my garments.[12]

Can you Tell the Real from the Counterfeit?

One of my first jobs was in Wilmington, Delaware as a teller in a large bank. They sent me on a seminar to learn about counterfeit money. Part way through the course, I raised my hand and asked,

WE DON'T KEEP FUNNY MONEY AT THIS BANK, THAT WOULD BE AN OXYMORON IF WE HAD COUNTERFEIT MONEY.

"When do we get to see counterfeit money?" The instructor said, "We don't have any counterfeit money. Actually, this course is not about acquainting you with the counterfeit, but the real currency. Our philosophy is that, if you're sufficiently familiar with the real currency, you'll spot anything that is different." A few months later, I was counting $20 bills and snapped up one of the bills, because it just did not look right. As I examined it, I concluded that it was a counterfeit. I showed it to a bank officer. He was not totally convinced. He asked me why I thought it was counterfeit. My response was: "There is too much shrubbery around the White House. I think the one who made these plates, loved gardening and decided to remedy the problem he saw in DC, by adding a few extra shrubs around the President's home." We sent it to the Money Room and they confirmed that it was, in fact, a counterfeit bill.

Don't be tempted to put on airs[13], or to be less than real, just to impress anyone. It is not worth being caste as a counterfeit. One way you can be real is to always be kind.[14] Sugar attracts more than vinegar ever will. Another way you can be real is to bring out the best in others, by affirming them, complimenting them, and encouraging them to look beyond themselves for what they can do to be a blessing and to pass it forward[15], rather than to see life for what it can give to them.[16] And, one more thing: Being real doesn't always mean giving a scathing review for a place of business, when well deserved. It may have been a bad day, meaning you may not have all the facts. Do let kindness and grace prevail, if at all possible. One Italian pastor, affirmed his own honesty, by saying, "There is no hair on my tongue."[17] Certainly businesses depend and hope for favorable reviews, and you should give them, when you can. However, when giving a review, do yourself a favor and dull your sharp tongue before typing out that review. Remember, "if you live by the sword, you will die by the sword."[18] In other words, if you are unkind and unreasonably difficult, then, at some point, in another place, that whirlwind of unkindness will be returned to you. Then the harvest will not be any better for you.

Don't Live your Life with Regrets, or You'll Regret it!

When in the last quarter of life, many discover that, for all their lives they have not been true to themselves and they have failed to address some of their more personal dreams. They could have done more; lived stronger, laughed harder, and been better stewards of the relationships they had with friends. It is always better to display more generosity, kindness, care, and love. To be disappointed with who you were, at a time when you can do little or nothing about it, is a difficult dilemma to face. Consider what choices you can make today to prepare yourself so that you could better face your last days with better answers than you might have today, if you were about to breathe your last breath. It takes courage to remain true to who you are.

Endnotes_____

1. Merriam-webster.com/dictionary - Real -not imaginary; not fake, false, or artificial; important and deserving to be regarded or treated in a serious way; not artificial, fraudulent, or illusory, being precisely what the name implies.

2. Merriam-webster.com/dictionary - Feigned - to pretend to feel or be affected by

3. www.Digital.library.upenn.edu - *The Velveteen Rabbit or How Toys Become Real* - The original story and illustrations as they first appeared in 1922, will work its magic for all who read it. Nursery magic is very strange and wonderful, and only those playthings that are old and wise and experienced like the Skin Horse understand all about it. Like the Skin Horse, Margery Williams understood how toys--and people--become real through the wisdom and experience of love.

4. www.charismamag.com/site-archives - Charisma Magazine - "Judson Cornwall (15 August 1924 – 11 February 2005) was a prolific Charismatic Christian preacher, pastor, and author of over 50 books on varied subjects such as worship, praise, spiritual warfare, and death." I spoke with Judson by phone a few weeks before he passed. He was a "Real" man of God and genuine in every way.

5. www.barrypopik.com/index.php/new_york_city/entry/jacques_penne - JC Penney, a department store, was founded by James Cash Penney in 1902 in Kemmerer, Wyoming. The faux French nickname of "Jacques Penné" for "J. C. Penney" has been cited in print since at least 1954, but became popular in the 1990s.

6. Matthew 25:14-30, especially verse 15 KJV - "And unto one he gave five talents, to another two, and to another one; to every man according to his several ability; and straightway took his journey."

7. Romans 12:3 NKJV "For I say, through the grace given to me, to everyone who is among you, not to think of himself more highly than he ought to think, but to think soberly, as God has dealt to each one a measure of faith."

8. www.en.wikipedia.org - Rubik's Cube is a 3-D combination puzzle invented in 1974 by Hungarian sculptor and professor of sculptor and professor of architecture Ernő Rubik. Although it is widely reported that the Cube was built as a teaching tool to help his students understand 3D objects, his actual purpose was solving the structural problem of moving the parts independently without the entire mechanism falling apart. He did not realize that he had created a puzzle until the first time he scrambled his new Cube and then tried to restore it.

9. Herr Ernst Kersten, an accomplished Potter of Kandern, Germany in the Black Forest. He was our landlord during the years of 1992-1994.

10. www.en.wikipedia.org - Anagama kiln - The Anagama kiln is an ancient type of pottery kiln brought to Japan from China via Korea in the 5th century. The Anagama is fuelled with firewood, in contrast to the electric or gas-fuelled kilns commonly used by most contemporary potters.

11. Daniel 3:19-26 MSG "Nebuchadnezzar, his face purple with anger... ordered the furnace fired up seven times hotter than usual. He ordered... Shadrach, Meshach, and Abednego, bound hand and foot, fully dressed from head to toe, were pitched into the roaring fire. Because the king was in such a hurry and the furnace was so hot, flames from the furnace killed the men who carried Shadrach, Meshach, and Abednego to it, while the fire raged around Shadrach, Meshach, and Abednego. Suddenly King Nebuchadnezzar jumped up in alarm and said, 'Didn't we throw three men, bound hand and foot, into the fire?' ... 'But look!' he said. 'I see four men, walking around freely in the fire, completely unharmed! And the fourth man looks like a son of the gods!' Nebuchadnezzar went to the door of the roaring furnace and called in, 'Shadrach, Meshach, and Abednego, servants of the High God, come out here!' Shadrach, Meshach, and Abednego walked out of the fire."

12. Revelation 3:5 NKJV "He who overcomes shall be clothed in white garments, and I will not blot out his name from the Book of Life; but I will confess his name before My Father and before His angels."

13. Thefreedictionary.com - Put on airs - to act better than one really is, to pretend to be good or to be superior.

14. www.goodreads.com/quotes/tag/being-real "Insecurity was never humility; just as arrogance was never success." Shannon L. Alder.

15. www.payitforwardday.com - Many of you may have seen the movie 'Pay It Forward' or have read the novel of the same name, a story about a young boy who did 3 good deeds for others in need. In return, all that the child wanted was that they pass on the good deed to three other people and keep the cycle going.

16. www.goodreads.com/quotes/tag/being-real - "You have fun at the cool kids table. I prefer my spot over here with the real people." Dan Pearce, Single Dad Laughing

17. www.italylogue.com/about-italy/italian-idiomatic-expressions - ***Italian Idiomatic Expressions:*** "The idea this phrase is meant to get across is that "He/she speaks his/her mind." But rather than say it so literally, the Italians have come up with a more interesting way of indicating this. The phrase above literally translates to "He/she doesn't have hairs on his/her tongue." No hairs on the tongue presumably means there's nothing to get in the way when someone's opinions roll downhill from the brain!"

18. en.wikipedia.org/wiki - "Live by the sword, die by the sword" is a saying of Jesus quoted in the Bible (See Matt. 26:52), to the effect that if you use violence, or other harsh means, against other people, you can expect to have those same means used against you; "You can expect to become a victim of whatever means you use to get what you want."

Is There a Grandfather in the House?

Chapter 16

Now is the Time to Reinvent Yourself
Realign, Refocus, Redirect

Today is possibly the best time for you to reinvent[1] or redefine yourself. To reinvent is to realign your life and ministry with your original call and to draw from talents God has given you over the years. So often, these are talents, which you have neglected to use. You have been the old you[2] for a very long time and now change[3] just may be the best thing for you. Some words, which may be of help, are: refocus, realign, redirect, refresh, rebirth[4], revamp, reawaken, renew, restate and reinvent. You may need to go back to the potter and take a few turns on the potter's wheel.

It has been great being so predictable that people know just when you will have your lunch, when you'll go to bed, when you'll get up and whether you will have your coffee at 8am and hot tea at 10am. It is amazing, when your associates can predict the answers you'd give, if certain questions were asked, or the jokes you would crack when situations come up. Think about this statement: Staying the same may not be your best compliment. Yes, "Jesus Christ is the same yesterday today and forever,"[5] but don't allow yourself to be guilty, as a human being who is growing and responding, loving, and experiencing your own renaissance, to fall into that uncreative mode where you become so predictable. In its own way, predictability can become a sort of pride, and such personal characteristics need to be approached with caution.

You're Almost There, but Not Quite There Yet

Why do I need to reinvent myself? Do I really need to experience a remake? Should I ask the Lord for a redefining moment? You may think you're perfect just as you are; you may feel that "God did a pretty good job on making me who I am," but read this poem by Shel Silverstein[6]:

"ALMOST PERFECT... BUT NOT QUITE." THOSE WERE THE WORDS OF MARY HUME AT HER SEVENTH BIRTHDAY PARTY, LOOKING 'ROUND THE RIBBONED ROOM. " THIS TABLECLOTH IS PINK NOT WHITE–ALMOST PERFECT... BUT NOT QUITE."

"ALMOST PERFECT... BUT NOT QUITE." THOSE WERE THE WORDS OF GROWN-UP MARY TALKING ABOUT HER HANDSOME BEAU, THE ONE SHE WASN'T GONNA MARRY. " SQUEEZES ME A BIT TOO TIGHT–ALMOST PERFECT... BUT NOT QUITE."

"ALMOST PERFECT... BUT NOT QUITE." THOSE WERE THE WORDS OF OL' MISS HUME TEACHING IN THE SEVENTH GRADE, GRADING PAPERS IN THE GLOOM LATE AT NIGHT UP IN HER ROOM. "THEY NEVER CROSS THEIR T'S JUST RIGHT– ALMOST PERFECT... BUT NOT QUITE."

NINETY-EIGHT THE DAY SHE DIED COMPLAININ'
'BOUT THE SPOTLESS FLOOR. PEOPLE SHOOK THEIR
HEADS AND SIGHED, "GUESS THAT SHE'LL LIKE HEAVEN
MORE." UP WENT HER SOUL ON FEATHERED WINGS, OUT
THE DOOR, UP OUT OF SIGHT. ANOTHER VOICE FROM
HEAVEN CAME– "ALMOST PERFECT... BUT NOT QUITE."

Most would agree that Mary Hume, in this poem, could have enriched her life a lot more, if she had been more flexible and tolerant of the ways of those around her, instead of putting herself up as the standard, to which all must conform.

NOW IS YOUR CHANCE. HAVE YOU EVER SAID, "IF I COULD JUST START OVER?"

To even entertain reinventing yourself may seem superficial or plastic, unreal or like tampering with the real you on the inside. I am not suggesting that you copy others or become someone you are not, but maybe you have missed something, which God has been trying to speak to you about for a long time. A blind spot may have developed and you have, in your busyness just carried on with life. You have buried so many instinctive inspirations under the layers of who you think you really are, but God wants to uncover and bring to light those urgings from so long ago. Could it be that you are more than what you see when you look into the mirror? We would all agree that your CV or resume will never give a fully accurate picture of all you're capable of being.

The Paul and Eleanor Stern Story

Paul and Eleanor Stern began their ministry together in 1949, as they prepared to serve the Lord in a cross-cultural work, which can only be called, missions to the world. Leaving their home church of Bethesda Missionary Temple, in Detroit, MI, they set their sights on Africa. Their 63 years of working together in ministry took them into long-term commitments in Kenya, Nigeria, and Eastern Europe. At one point they pastored a church in Danville, Illinois for 16 years.

The first time I met Paul was at the "Washington for Jesus Rally" on April 29, 1980, where approximately 500,000[7] believers from all across America came together on the Washington Monument Mall to celebrate Jesus. Pastors John and Ann Giminez, of Rock Church, Virginia Beach, VA, had organized this event. At the time I was pastoring in Decatur, GA and Paul was one of the dignitaries on the huge platform.

When Paul and Eleanor were in Detroit, MI and were being ordained for ministry, in a ceremony, they received an impromptu Prophetic Word by one of the presbytery team. Essentially, this is the word, which came to them on that day: "God will send you to a place He has already placed in your hearts." Even then they knew that place would be Africa. It continued stating clearly that Eleanor would be a "Mother in an orphanage." Clearly the focus was on Eleanor that day. The years passed and she occasionally thought of that word, but she was still young.

GOD REALLY CAN SEE INTO THE FUTURE AND HE CAN DO MIRACLES TOO.

Finally, in 2001, while in a prayer service at Nairobi Lighthouse Church, the Holy Spirit touched Eleanor's heart as she was reading from the Bible where it says, "For the life of your young children, who faint from hunger at the head of every street."[8] The Holy Spirit had been dealing with her occasionally all through the years. Now she took personal inventory, realizing that she was no longer as young as she had been before, and that God was using this verse to prompt her attention back to the idea of an orphanage.

Now Eleanor found herself saying, "After all these years, at my age, are you calling me to start an orphanage?" This is what she heard deep within her spirit on that evening: "Sarah was 90 years old when I called her to care for a child.[9] I am not asking you to give physical birth to any children." Somehow, that was a relief to Eleanor, that all she had to do was care for the children.

> TO IMPROVE IS TO CHANGE, TO BE PERFECT IS TO CHANGE OFTEN.

Eleanor and Paul went back to the USA to live for a while. Then she heard the prompting of the Lord again saying, "You won't be able to establish an orphanage in Africa, while sitting in America." That is when the Sterns made a decision and began preparation to make, yet another international move. They closed down their home and determined to move back to Kenya to walk in obedience, arriving in Nairobi in 2002. Over the next two years they did the following:

* Selected the site for building King's Kids Village

* Purchased the 5 acres of prime land for a price of US $162,000.00.

* Churches and friends joined to back them for this venture and to help them begin immediately to pay off the debt and begin construction.

* The rest of 2002 and through May of 2004 was spent building a two story building with four huge apartments, which now houses four group homes, each with a couple to serve as house parents.

* On opening day they received two little boys and the first set of house parents.

* In 2015 the property has escalated in value to US $5,000,000 and they are debt free.

* In 2015 King's Kids Village has 39 kids on campus and 8 in transition toward adulthood.

* They have since built an education center.

* And are now building "transition housing" for the older kids who are in transition into adulthood.

Several years ago, while ministering in Kenya, we visited the Stern's and their orphanage. We were impressed with the Excellency of all they had built. It has been a pleasure ministering with Paul and Eleanor in Kenya, Germany and also in Budapest, Hungary. Paul even came to our aid, being proficient in German, when we were filing the paperwork to take up residency in Germany ourselves.

When the Sterns came to agreement on retiring from active duty, they realized they must choose a successor. Their son, Jon, and his wife, Molly, had been serving as missionaries in Kenya already. This was a natural transition for Jon and Molly and so, they made the necessary commitments and moved into the place of directors of the Home. Paul and Eleanor moved back to America and then, in 2013 Paul passed into the presence of the Lord. Eleanor has just moved back, once again, to Nairobi to remain there indefinitely.

I find it interesting that Eleanor has just published a book, entitled, "Never Too Old."[10] At the time of this writing, she can be classified as vintage, at the age of 88. She is such a treasure to all who know her. Eleanor is doing well, has always been strong, and continues even to today, having just arrived back at her adopted homeland of Kenya to look over the kids. Surely she is the "Mother in a great orphanage."

Hop Up Onto the Potter's Wheel For a Remake

Take a look at what happened to Jeremiah and think instead, that it's happening to you. Of course, in this conversation the one on the potter's wheel was the nation of Israel, but let's imagine that it is "you" on the wheel, today.

Please read Jeremiah 18:1-4 and then sit back and listen to the Holy Spirit as He speaks to you. "Go down to the potter's shop, and I will speak to you there."[11] So I went to the potter's house, and sure enough, the potter was there, working away at his wheel. Whenever the pot, the potter was working on, turned out badly, as sometimes happens when you are working with clay, the potter would simply start over and use the same clay to make another pot."[12]

It is time to reinvent yourself, so that you will remain viable into the future. You cannot grow without embracing change, or redefining yourself. The world is in a constant state of change, in thoughts, culture, lifestyle, and world-view. It is not our purpose, in this writing, to validate the ways the world is changing, or even to identify if they're going down a wrong path. The idea here is that change is inevitable and you are living in a wind tunnel[13] and a fast changing world. Few things are the same in the 21st century, as they were in the 20th century. Just like the courses in a brick building, you must grow one layer at a time. Growth is not the mastery of staying the same, but evolving into new perceptions, new perspectives, and the ability to deal with being refashioned.

HOPE WE RECOGNIZE YOU WHEN YOU GET THROUGH WITH YOUR FACELIFT!

It is my opinion that, in order to stretch out, expand, and mature, you must learn to reinvent yourself and who you are at least every 4-6 years. The call will remain the same, but the way you respond to that call has to shift as new doors, new insights and circumstances come into view. Otherwise, you run the risk of growing stale and complacent. You only have one life to live, so approach every day with the zest to live it to the fullest.

Do Not Blame Your Family for Your Failure to Obey

There is one principle that fits well with this point in our study and one, which you will do well to embrace. You must never use your spouse, or your family, or your finances as an excuse for why you cannot follow the leading of the Holy Spirit. If the Spirit leads you, then He will make a way. The question is regarding your will to obey, or to follow his lead, not to mention the courage required to take a step of faith. Please allow me to give you some examples from our lives.

We were pastoring a church in Georgia, USA. Our son and daughter were small, and I felt that I should pursue a teaching ministry, which would require lots of travel. It was never a consideration, that I would travel alone, maintaining a home in a central place for my family to stay, leaving me to come and go. This would minimize my access and input into my family. It would put a strain on the relationship I enjoyed with my wife, and would reduce my influence in the lives of our son and daughter. Traveling alone would be unwise. As a minister, I would be vulnerable and unprotected. Besides, I am a family man, and like to have my family with me at all times. After that was established, my wife and I realized that, if we were to pursue this venture, we must make the following commitments. We chose to live in an RV[14], we would move often and home school the children, as I conducted workshops and seminars throughout the continental United States and six of the Canadian provinces.

My wife, Christi, is ever the willing participant when it comes to adventure. She has been aptly armed with a tolerance for risk, strong faith to step out of the boat, and a powerful prayer life.[15] We decided that this step of faith would require a total revamping of how we saw ourselves. We gave our notice to the church and went on our way. It would be about three months before we could obtain a 25 ft. travel trailer, but we kept praying, and it came in the right time. Until then we stayed in temporary quarters, hotels, motels, church apartments, and homes. People were kind to us, patient, generous, and loving. We were fulfilled and energized.

THERE CHRISTI STOOD, WITH HER BACKPACK ON AND READY TO LAUNCH, I MARRIED THE RIGHT GIRL.

Although this chapter lasted four years, we were praying during those years for South Africa, and the challenges in that part of the world, still not having learned to connect the dots.[16] We had learned the principle that it is good practice to include into our list of prayer subjects, the commitment to pray for some other field, which lies outside of our own world. In our case, we had been praying for the nation of South Africa, and all that was transpiring there half way around the world. It took several chapters and transitions to realize that there was a pattern forming, and the Lord wanted us to reinvent ourselves as a part of our rhythm. We were slow at first, to find our rhythm, but eventually we learned to dance.

Four years passed, several travel trailers later, and lots of great picnics in state parks; and we began to feel the nudging of the Holy

Spirit for a change in direction. We understood what motivated Paul, the Apostle, and what he faced, along with so many others, who worked at building the church in earlier times. We grasped what their commitment level had to be and asked the Holy Spirit to fashion our lives accordingly. We experienced unique opportunities to hear the voice of the Lord. The day came and we moved from scheduled speaking engagements in North American cities to establishing a home in South Africa, and the town of Amanzimtoti, near the city of Durban. In the township of Kwamakhutha we assumed the position of principal to give direction to the Zulu Bible College. This was a challenge and a fantastic change for us, and one, which would leave us with excellent memories.

We lived in South Africa for six years, working with a Zulu Bible school and ministering all through the nation. We loved that nation and were content to continue working there for many years to come, having no thoughts about the possibility of leaving.

AFTER YOU HAVE EMBARKED ON YOUR ASSIGNMENTS, YOU MAY NEED TO MAKE OCCASIONAL CORRECTIONS TO THE COORDINATES!

One day I was finished work and had an epiphany from the Holy Spirit, just before going home. In my heart I knew instantly, by the nature of this visitation, that we were released from that field of ministry. I arrived at home, and shared the experience with my wife, without giving her any indication as to what I felt the vision meant to me. Then I asked her what she felt it meant to her? She immediately said, "I believe, without question, that the Lord has released us from our work here." Within four months we transitioned out of South Africa and into Europe. Living in Germany we met up with new challenges, but God was faithful and we learned to bend with whatever the Lord required. The key to our lives has become flexibility.

How Often Should I Go Through a Redefining Process?

We all go through cycles, seasons of life, and chapter changes. There are no hard fast rules as to the timing of these life-altering experiences. We are all different, from our unique personalities, different assignments, and even the cultures in which we live.

The cycles of the Bishop family have lasted, strangely enough, about four to six years. We obviously have a more mobile calling than many others. Ours is not the standard for all to follow, for sure, but merely, the pattern we must follow for our lives and ministry. We have felt, at various intervals, the strong unction of the Lord to pray for a part of the world, or a particular region. We would engage in this prayer exercise for several years, without realizing that it had anything to do with what our next step should be. Only after the passing of long periods of time, did it become clear that the Holy Spirit was moving us into, yet another transition. As you can see, we have embraced the way God has directed us. I realize men who are in denominations with a strong hierarchy in place over them, would not have the flexibility we have enjoyed. Still, it is vital that everyone thinks outside of the box, and exercises freedom to follow the Spirit's leading as they receive His direction. I realize that I am speaking for our family, and yet, there are ways you can also reinvent yourself if you realize the benefits.

When it comes to redefining yourself, do not embrace the Popeye perspective, as he sang that song in that much publicized

BE LIKE A RENAISSANCE MAN. IT'S TIME TO REMOLT LIKE THE EAGLE.

cartoon, "I yam what I yam, and that's all that I yam."[16] It may sound self confident, but it also sounds unchanging, unbending and just too rigid. The mighty oak may appear ideal, but to be able to bend like the palm tree just may fit you better, as you carry on in this changing world, allowing yourself an occasional makeover in your effort to remain relevant to the generations of your day.

Endnotes_____

1. dictionary.reference.com/browse/reinvent?s=t ~ verb. "To reinvent again or anew, especially without knowing that the invention already exists. To bring back; revive." To realign what you do with your original call and to draw out talents God has given you over the years. Staying the same is not a compliment.

2. dictionary.reference.com/browse/you ~ "the nature or character of the person   addressed." Try to discover the hidden you.

3. www.merriam-webster.com/dictionary/change ~ Change: To undergo a modification.

4. John 1:12-13 NLT ~ "But to all who believed him and accepted him, he gave the right to become children of God. They are reborn—not with a physical birth resulting from human passion or plan, but a birth that comes from God." Consider that the rebirth you can experience (which is from God), may be on several levels, not only to become RE-BORN, in the spirit, but also in your use of talents the Lord has given to you.

5. Hebrews 13:8 KJV ~"Jesus Christ is the same yesterday, today, and forever."

6. En.wikipedia.org/wiki ~ Sheldon Allan "Shel" Silverstein (September 25, 1930 – May 10, 1999) was an American poet, singer-songwriter, cartoonist, screenwriter, and author of children's books. He styled himself as Uncle Shelby in some works. Translated into more than 30 languages, his books have sold over 20 million copies.

7. en.wikipedia.org/wiki/Washington_for_Jesus

8. Lamentations 2:19 NIV

9. Genesis 17:17 NIV "Abraham fell facedown; he laughed and said to himself, "Will a son be born to a man a hundred years old? Will Sarah bear a child at the age of ninety?"

10. Book: _"Never Too Old"_ by Eleanor L. Stern. Available on Amazon.com ISBN: 9781512319644

11. Jeremiah 18:2 NLT

12. Jeremiah 18:1-4 MSG "God told Jeremiah, 'Up on your feet! Go to the potter's house. When you get there, I'll tell you what I have to say.' So I went to the potter's house, and sure enough, the potter was there, working away at his wheel. Whenever the pot the potter was working on turned out badly, as sometimes happens when you are working with clay, the potter would simply start over and use the same clay to make another pot."

13. The American Heritage Science Dictionary ~ wind tunnel ~ A chamber through which air is blown at controlled speeds to simulate the motion of objects placed in the chamber through the air, used to study the aerodynamic properties of objects such as automobiles, airplanes, and missiles.

14. RV ~ Recreational Vehicle: in our case, a travel trailer, pulled behind our vehicle.

15. Matthew 14:29 NKJV "So He said, 'Come.' And when Peter had come down out of the boat, he walked on the water to go to Jesus."

16. Dictionary.com - Idiom: To connect the dots - "To draw a conclusion from disparate (or different) facts." Learning to connect bits of information so that you can see the bigger picture.

17. Wikipedia.org/wiki/I_Yam_What_I_Yam - "The Paramount Pictures cartoon series: "Popeye the Sailor." It was the 2nd cartoon in the cartoon series that lasted from 1933-1957. The star was "William "Billy" Costello as Popeye." As much as I realize that this cartoon is very old, it is a part of our Pop History and worth mentioning.

Chapter 17

What Shall It Be? Will I Retire or Refire?

Find a New and Unique Door of Ministry for You

Facing a new life chapter may open up for you new options you have not considered. The big question is often, should I retire or re-fire? This word, "re-fire" is not exactly found in the dictionary, as much as it does relate to when a fire has gone out and re-ignites to produce even more effect, extending the influence of the original fire. Jeremiah made reference to the anointing in his life, as "a fire shut up in my bones."[1]

At issue here is what are you to do when you come to the place when society's expectations are that you stop your day-job and do something different. It really depends on who you have become and what your hopes and dreams are at that time. Granted, health issues, etc. can place limitations upon you, but even so, you may still find that there remains hope for new commitments and new paths of service for the kingdom of God. At such times, the big question becomes: "Do I retire… take a bow and exit the stage of ministry?" or "do I look for new and unique doors of ministry or service?"

One More Question Before You Respond

Are you married? How is your wife in all that you are considering? How has she faired, after all those years of ministry? Would you say that she needs a break, a vacation, a sabbatical, or a total change? Is she longing to retire? How is her health? Would you do well to take her away for a while to breathe different air and take personal inventory as to what the next step should be, for her, as well as you? Have you prayed a lot together about what lies before you both?

This lady has stood with you, walked with you, served with you, sacrificed with you. She has been one flesh[2] with you and now, is continuing your journey wherever it takes you. There is a strong case for thinking that you would be called upon to yield and hear her thoughts, on issues that are so important at this time? She has been wise so often and may even hold the keys to a better life chapter. For faithfully standing with you for umpteen[3] years, your wife is also in a place where honor is due to her, and likely even double honor.

You would be wise, to answer no more of my questions, until you have brought her into the loop on what her opinions might be. My suggestion is that, even if you feel you have heard her out, take time to ask the appropriate questions and then sit back for a while and listen to whatever she feels to say. When she has stopped talking, keep quiet, because she probably has more to say. Then, when she is finished, don't give your opinion, but pray together and make your decisions together. Don't make the decisions yourself, but draw her in strongly to the process.

My Own Story of Unique Opportunities

I have been married to Christina Reed Bishop since 1970. We have been in the ministry our entire married life. Thirty years ago, we went on our first mission assignment and have lived in five other nations since that time. In 2014 we made a move to the Republic of Ireland. Although I am not retired, and do not plan that move for some time to come, I am getting closer to that time, and can certainly relate to making ministry and life changes as it becomes necessary.

My ministry has been that of a missionary, pastor, writer, preacher and teacher. I have served as mentor and Life Coach to those God has brought across my path.

In Ireland there are not as many Evangelical, Spirit filled, or protestant churches as in so many other nations where we have worked. I have taught in many Bible School settings, as well as conducted leadership-training conferences in many nations. We met with quite a number of pastors throughout Ireland and Northern Ireland, but were still faced with the challenge on what could we do to make a solid contribution to building the church, with Christ. What would be our assignment, while here? We prayed for open doors that would fit our cross-cultural skills. I was especially praying for unique open doors of ministry. It was at that time that we were introduced to Colin and Sunhwa Jenkins.[4] Colin works with the Seamen's Christian Friends Society, and holds the title of Cork Port Chaplain for Cork City and Cobh Harbor. Colin invited me to join him when possible, as he was on-board the huge commercial ships, including cargo ships,

> IF YOU CAN THINK OUTSIDE THE BOX, THEN HALF THE QUESTIONS ARE ANSWERED.

container ships, oil tankers and even cruise ships, which come to the harbor daily, from around the world. The crews and officers of these ships welcome those who are willing to take a personal interest in them, as well as to minister to them; this usually results in times of Bible teaching and prayer.

One of my open, and certainly unique doors of opportunity came in the form of this ministry to the Seafarers. Although this is not what I usually do, it does encompass my mission vision, because I love ministering cross-culturally and feel a mandate for world missions. Many of the sailors I have met and ministered to, are from nations I've visited in our travels around the globe. This has given me immediate rapport with so many of them, as I can speak to them easily. Going into the huge commercial ships to convey the Gospel was a brand new open door for me, and one, which I never anticipated.

Let me tell you a little about these men. There are 1.5 million seafarers, mostly men, on these ships, comprised of men from over 100 nations. According to the SCFS website 90% of all trade passes through the 6,000 commercial seaports in the world, and about 80,000 merchant ships traverse the globe to make that happen. Nearly every ship is manned by several different nationalities. Over half of these come from the Philippines. The common language spoken on-board is English, so that certainly is a benefit for me. Most of these men are contracted for 9-10 months at a time, taking them home only about 2-3 months to be with their families, before leaving to join another ship. In a 6-year period a seafarer may only spend a total of 1 year at home with his family, resulting in their spending about 85% of their working lives at sea. Contact with their families is infrequent because of the high cost of satellite communications. Times in port are usually brief, with few opportunities to even go ashore. Whether at sea or in port, seafarers work 10-12 hours a day for 6-7 days each week.[5]

Many of these seafarers come from nations, which do not allow them freedom of religion. As a result, if I were in their home country, I would likely be unable to speak to them freely about Jesus Christ. However, when they board these commercial ships, all the rules change and they often become open to Christianity and the Gospel. If they receive the Lord into their lives, then the hope is that they'll take this message to their families and friends, so that the Kingdom of God is expanded into hostile nations. I really do love it "when a plan comes together."[6]

Although we are engaged in other areas of ministry in this nation, work with the Seafarers has become one of my favorite focuses.

How to Find New and Creative Ways to Minister

What have been your life's dreams and those things, which have interested you most? If you have answers that come to you quite naturally, then that is good. But if that is not the case, then go on a journey in your heart to search for what God would lead you to consider.

Pray about and go looking for a new and unique door of ministry that you could pursue for the Kingdom of God

Some Ideas You Might Consider Would Be:

* First of all, seek the Lord for His will for the balance of your life.

* Become a chaplain to a Convalescent Home or hospital.

* Find a youth group or sports club in your city, which needs mentors.

* If you are proficient in another language, become an interpreter with the local court system.[7]

* Spend time with the inmates at the city, county, state, provincial or federal prisons.

STEP NUMBER 1:
ASK GOD FOR
DIRECTION

* Teach classes or do some mentoring at the local Rehabilitation Center.

* Find creative way to affirm and encourage former soldiers who are "Wounded Warriors"

STEP NUMBER
2: LISTEN FOR
THE ANSWER

* Should you be so fortunate as to be near a Refugee Center, then take time to reach out to those who are staying there. This will be a cross-cultural challenge for you.

* If you are good at appliance repairs, painting or woodworking then help single mothers or widows.

* Seek out a church where you could become a "care pastor" to help lift the load of the lead pastor.

* Teach a Bible class in a church.

* Take up cooking or find open doors to your hospitality skills. After all, the Bible says to be given to hospitality.[8] How could you utilize this gift in such a way as to invest in your local community?[9]

* Get involved with an inner city ministry.

* Go on a mission trip to another nation, or the Native American reservations. Today they're often called, "First Nations People."

- Find a local radio station and talk to the management about how you would like to have 3 or so broadcasting slots each week, taking 10-15 minutes to just tell stories of the goodness of Jesus, or tell the stories of miracles in the Bible. They may not even charge you for the time on the air. Do it like a "fireside chat," not in a preachy manner, but just talk like a grandfather who is talking to the family.

- Get engaged with Sowers International. They're a good group and do many good things for mission projects of various types.[10]

- Write a book, or even your memoirs. What are your interests to write about?

- Take a class in creative writing, or painting.

- Learn to play a musical instrument, or learn a language.

- Explore your possibilities and do it today.

The objective is to find a new and unique way of ministry, which will bring fulfilment and divine opportunity.

Endnotes

1. Jeremiah 20:9 NKJV Then I said, "I will not make mention of Him, nor speak anymore in His name. But His word was in my heart like a burning fire shut up in my bones; I was weary of holding it back, and I could not."

2. Genesis 2:23 MSG "The Man said, 'Finally! Bone of my bone, flesh of my flesh! Name her Woman for she was made from Man.' Therefore a man leaves his father and mother and embraces his wife. They become one flesh. The two of them, the Man and his Wife, were naked, but they felt no shame."

3. Dictionary.reference.com/browse/umpteen ~ "innumerable; many years." Almost too many years to count.

4. www.scfs.org/supporters/ports/cork/ ~ Colin & Sunhwa Jenkins ~ They began work as the Cork Port Chaplains at the beginning of September 2006. This work is a unique pastoral and mission-focused ministry. Colin tells how he has met seafarers from over 20 nations already. These men have been atheists, agnostics, Hindus, Muslims, Greek and Russian Orthodox, Buddhists and Christians. This ministry has opened the door for sharing the love of Jesus with them, as well as often loading them up in his car and taking them to church services. Colin even is often seen transporting the ship cooks to buy groceries for the ship's crew. He truly has shown himself to be a servant of love to these men of the seas.

5. www.scfs.org.au/scfs/index.php ~ *The Seamen's Christian Friend Society* is an interdenominational Christian mission that is committed to "Taking the Message of Life to Seafarers." Note: The seafarers hail from over 100 nations, with a majority of them from the Philippines.

6. www.youtube.com/watch?v=FPQlXNH36mI ~ In the TV series, "A-Team" the lead character, Hannibal Smith's theme line was: "I love it when a plan comes together."

7. One of my friends, Pastor Buddy Holder, in Logansport, Indiana is proficient in Spanish. There are a lot of Latinos who have moved into his area. Often they have court cases, which require a translator or an interpreter. Buddy has found a beautiful place of ministry among the foreigners.

8. 1 Timothy 3:2 NLT "So an elder must be a man whose life is above reproach. He must be faithful to his wife. He must exercise self-control, live wisely, and have a good reputation. He must enjoy having guests in his home, and he must be able to teach." Note that "Hospitality" could be expanded to include more than just in his home, but a teachable moment could be seized upon to have an effective new and vibrant open door, because most of us get hungry quite often. Think about it!

9. Matthew 25:34-40 MSG "Then the King will say to those on his right, 'Enter, you who are blessed by my Father! Take what's coming to you in this kingdom. It's been ready for you since the world's foundation. And here's why: I was hungry and you fed me, I was thirsty and you gave me a drink, I was homeless and you gave me a room, I was shivering and you gave me clothes, I was sick and you stopped to visit, I was in prison and you came to me. Then those 'sheep' are going to say, 'Master, what are you talking about? When did we ever see you hungry and fed you, thirsty and gave you a drink? And when did we ever see you sick or in prison and came to you?' Then the King will say, 'I'm telling the solemn truth: Whenever you did one of these things to someone overlooked or ignored, that was me—you did it to me."

10. www.sowersinternational.com - We Are Local Church Bodies around the world, made up of people like yourselves, partnering and volunteering their time, energies and prayers.

Is There a Grandfather in the House?

Chapter 18

PRESS INTO YOUR CREATIVE SIDE (PART 1)
A NEW OPEN DOOR, SERENDIPITY, DIVINE OPPORTUNITY

All your life you have had your own way of doing things. You've used a certain number of your gifts and talents, but now, at this new juncture in your life, God may choose to open doors, which are more creative opportunities and something entirely different than anything you have ever done before. Wisdom would dictate to you at this time to prepare for growth, get ready for new doors and new ventures, even when conventional wisdom would whisper that you are coming to an end and should start closing your doors and guarding your strength. Get ready and clear the ground around you for a new and creative mindset:

> "ENLARGE YOUR HOUSE; BUILD AN ADDITION.
> SPREAD OUT YOUR HOME, AND SPARE NO EXPENSE!
> FOR YOU WILL SOON BE BURSTING AT THE SEAMS.
> YOUR DESCENDANTS WILL OCCUPY OTHER
> NATIONS AND RESETTLE THE RUINED CITIES."[1]

There is an open door before you, but you must have your eyes and your spirit open to such things. If you cannot see the door, then it does not exist for you.

Many people can be classified as either too cautious or too impulsive. The rest of us fall somewhere in between these two extremes. The difference is often a fog, which distorts perspective. The fog, or the mist, may muddle your view and keep you from recognizing new and creative opportunities.[2] Everyone has had opportunities pass them by. The challenge is to recognize the open door and see its value, so that you can step through and allow it to change your life. "Physicists work under the assumption that there are at least 10 dimensions, but we will never 'see' them. Because we only know life in 3-D, our brains don't understand how to look for anything more. Our minds aren't trained to see anything other than our world, and it will likely take something from another dimension to make us understand."[3]

Life goes on without a lot of drama, until you are entering into a chapter change. During times of change, doors may appear, even though they may have been there all along. Keep your senses alive, your heart open, and you just may see a door that you have not expected. It could be your serendipity.[4]

HOW MANY DIMENSIONS HAVE YOU LIVED IN? HOW MANY ARE YOU WILLING TO TRY?

These become the times when you should double up on your prayer life, so that your spiritual ears can hear the inner voice of the Holy Spirit.

Pressing into your creative side, may be a lot easier than you think; but it may require a higher level of courage and adventure than you are accustomed to exercising. If you come from a mindset that will allow others' unique success, while not extending the same expectation to you, then you need to snap yourself out of the fog, or that hypnotic state of self-limitation. Note this: you are as worthy of success as anyone around you.

The Archie & Verna Alderson Story

I would like to share the story of what happened to my friends, who had been in Japan for over 30 years and involved in cross cultural work with the church. Here is their story.

Their life's work had gone well and the successes of establishing new churches had been good, but things seemed to be slowing down and they began to feel that changes of some kind were imminent for them. They had decided to expand into a new area and start one more church, which they would customarily pass to a national worker in due time. While looking for a venue they passed a lavishly designed chapel, where weddings were held. At that time, in Japan, there had developed a trend where "Western Christian Weddings" were all the rage. Many young, upwardly mobile couples were opting to pay lots of money and take the step to engage the directors of this chapel for their big day.

My friends, Archie and Verna Alderson, decided to stop by to ask if, perhaps, the management would consider renting out their chapel, when the building was not in use. The closer they got, the more reluctant Archie became to make the inquiry. However, Verna was energized and insisted that they be adventurous and hopeful, and so they did. Upon entering the establishment, the associate

> THIS IS A DREAM OFFER AND I NEVER REALIZED I WAS DREAMING, AND CERTAINLY NOT ABOUT THAT.

director especially enjoyed meeting this American couple and made a comment. "So, you are a Japanese speaking pastor from America? And you have been here for the last 30 years? I would like to suggest that our wedding chapel needs someone like you to perform our western style Christian weddings, on a regular basis. Actually, you would be perfect and the man who has been doing it is unable to continue. We have been looking for someone and you would be absolutely suitable for this work. I'd like to introduce you to the director."

This took the Alderson's aback, as they could not envision how this could be an acceptable adjustment in how they had always done things as missionaries. Several days passed, as they considered this new idea. Because of their extreme caution, the opportunity almost slipped away from them. Verna was excited and felt that this was a new ministry door and they should spring for it. Archie, however, remained cautious.

They were out shopping several days later. While sitting on a bench, at the mall, Archie heard a clear word from the Holy Spirit. He said, "It was so forceful, I knew immediately that I must respond." The still small voice of the Lord was so compelling, "Go now, and secure this opportunity. You are to do all they ask you to do. Now is the time to take a step." Not wanting to offend Japanese protocol for proper attire, he almost didn't go, because he was not dressed in a suit. But then there was the urgency in his spirit, so he went directly to the chapel office, without Verna. After all, he knew Verna was all in; it was he who had been dragging his feet.

This is what materialized for the Alderson's as they accepted this new and creative opportunity. For just over 13 years they conducted 3,300 Western style Christian weddings in this chapel. The decor was beautiful, with flowers, music and all fully in place. As Archie performed the ministerial duties for these weddings he was free to write the script as he wished. Although the general population of Japan was not Christian, they accepted that a Western style Christian wedding had its own culture and they'd gladly pay for it and accept it just as it came to them. The laws of Japan, as in so many other nations, require citizens to go to their local government office for a civil marriage certificate, after which they can elect to have a Shinto, or Western Christian wedding ceremony. No ceremony of any kind is required under Japanese law[5], but the trend is to go for a ceremony. This is when the beauty of this opportunity became clear to the Aldersons.

Soon it became evident that this new door brought with it even more benefits that complimented their lifelong mission vision. Archie was able to receive these couples into his office and give them proper Christian counseling, as to what it meant to be a Christian, the role Jesus played in the lives of a Christian couple, and how to accept Jesus as Lord of your life and marriage. He always concluded this counseling time with prayer, for them and for the marriage they were about to enter into. Then, in the wedding itself, Verna, with two back up singers, would sing songs like, "What a Friend we have in Jesus,"[6] and "Oh Perfect Love."[7] Verna always accompanied Archie and actually sang over 7000 times during those years. Nearly every time, when Verna sang these songs, tears would flow down the cheeks of the bride and bridesmaids. They could not help themselves. These songs evoked a response, as the Creator reached out and touched their hearts. Yes, this was a business, but it was a business that actually helped them expose more Japanese to the

TWO VETERAN MISSIONARIES BECOME CELEBRITIES IN JAPAN. THEY WERE ALL THE RAGE.

Kingdom of God than their former mission work. Not only were the participants exposed to the "Good News of Jesus Christ" but also each couple paid for a full video of everything that happened at this event. The tradition is then to show their precious video to all who come to visit them in their home, for years to come. The viewing of the video multiplied exponentially the exposure of the Japanese to Christianity. This trendy wedding opportunity brought Archie and Verna into contact with all of the social strata, which they had previously been unable to reach; doctors, lawyers, professors, business leaders, politicians, and even religious leaders of the nation.

There was one occasion when ten Buddhist priests were in attendance, and accepted all the proceedings without any criticism, because the Wedding Chapel had notified them in advance of the culture of a Christian Wedding.

This creative opportunity was a portal through which the Aldersons were able to navigate and accomplish new and unique things, which otherwise would not have been possible.

The Aldersons were still able to establish the new church in that city. They were so pleased because the Wedding Chapel Company donated the use of another nearby chapel for its use. Not only the building but also the complete utilities were available without cost for the entire 13 years. When the Aldersons repatriated back to San Antonio, Texas it was with joy. The generosity, which the company had shown in remunerating the Aldersons for their services, enabled them to purchase a beautiful new home and a new automobile, leaving them without debt. Their retirement was blessed because God took care of those 13 years in a creative way.

Live on the edge, and press into the new and creative opportunities, which may present themselves, while you are in the middle of your chapter changes. God is consistently working to open new doors for you to pass through. The challenge is to make every day a day when you are listening for his voice.

Do not assume that life will spiral downward into a narrow world of limitation and doubt. Remember this: God is for you and will work for you to help you. Note the words of this verse from the Message Bible: "God will lavish you with good things: children from your womb, offspring from your animals, and crops from your land, the land that God promised your ancestors that he would give you. God will throw open the doors of his sky vaults and pour rain on your land on schedule and bless the work you take in hand. You will lend to many nations but you yourself won't have to take out a loan. God will make you the head, not the tail; you'll always be the top dog, never the bottom dog, as you obediently listen to and diligently keep the commands of God, your God, that I am commanding you today. Don't swerve an inch to the right or left from the words that I command you today by going off following and worshiping other gods."[8]

> DON'T ASSUME YOU'LL FALL BETWEEN THE CRACKS. YOU ARE A CANDIDATE FOR "MISSION IMPOSSIBLE."

Read the same verses from New Living Translation: "If you listen to these commands of the Lord your God that I am giving you today, and if you carefully obey them, the Lord will make you the head and not the tail, and you will always be on top and never at the bottom."[9]

Endnotes

1. Isaiah 54:2-3 NLT

2. Dictionary.com ~ any darkened state of the atmosphere, or the diffused substance that causes it.

3. science.howstuffworks.com/science-vs-myth/everyday-myths/see-the-fourth-dimension. htm ~ Article: *Can our brains see the fourth dimension?* By Molly Edmonds

4. Wikipedia.org ~ Serendipity means a "fortunate happenstance" or "pleasant surprise."

5. Wikipedia.org ~ Marriage in Japan

6. library.timelesstruths.org/music ~ Lyrics of the Song: *"What a Friend we have in Jesus"*

7. www.oremus.org/hymnal/o/o517.html ~ Lyrics of the Song: *"Oh Perfect Love"*

8. Deuteronomy 28:13-14 MSG

9. Deuteronomy 28:13-14 NLT

Chapter 19

PRESS INTO YOUR CREATIVE SIDE (PART 2)
BE POISED TO MOVE WITH THE CLOUD

Pressing into your creative side is a challenge, which needs the attention of everyone who takes seriously the seasons of life. You may discover that one of your biggest tests is in simply how you respond to new and innovative open doors. If you do not blink, but rather get a sparkle in your eyes, then hold on, you may discover a new day and a new path. Of course many do not enjoy such challenges, and would rather maintain the status quo than press on new doors of opportunities. But, I realize that is not you. You are ready, willing and anticipating what may come your way. Please allow me to share my own personal mission statement:

> "LIFE'S JOURNEY IS NOT TO ARRIVE AT THE
> GRAVE SAFELY IN A WELL PRESERVED BODY, BUT
> RATHER TO SKID IN SIDEWAYS, TOTALLY WORN
> OUT SHOUTING, "WOW, WHAT A RIDE."[1]

The Russ and Lana Frase Story

Dr. Russ and Lana Frase[2] were happy, settled and loving the place they occupied in ministry, as director of a Bible school in the

BEWARE OF WHEN YOU ARE CONTENT ... COUNT TO TEN AND HOLD YOUR BREATH.

Midwest, under the banner of a larger church. At the age of 61, Dr. Frase was content with where he was in his ministry and career. After 20 years on staff with the church he felt his future was reasonably secure. He was fulfilled and confident. He especially enjoyed the two classrooms and his entire faculty.

In the midst of this, and unknowingly, Russ and Lana were about to enter a new phase of ministry. Things were about to change for them, and God had everything under control.

Things Changed for Russ and Lana

Word came down from the corporate leadership that, because of budgetary adjustments, this school would close at the end of the school year. This was certainly a disappointment to them. They realized that God would work for them, but, for a few days, it was a bit surreal. They had to remind themselves that God was not taken by surprise, but had a new path they should walk down.

The school had been in operation for 14 years. This closing would require all those involved in the school to seek new and alternative opportunities for expression of their ministries, and studies.

It was about that time that Dr. Frase found himself on a plane hearing the stewardess asking him to help her balance out the weight of the plane before take off. He was asked to move from his side of the plane to the other side and up a few seats to sit down beside a couple of total strangers. As he sat in his new seat assignment, he discovered this couple was Russ and Wendy Tatro[3], missionaries over the last 28 years in the African nations of Liberia and Cameroon. They began to talk about missions and the nations. It was then that Russ Tatro made an amazing offer: "I have a two year Bible curriculum in Spanish, complete with lectures and exams, that I would like to give to you." Dr. Frase said, "Well, we don't use Spanish or teach anything in Spanish at our Bible school," and politely let the Tatros know that he did not want to take it and then fail to live up to their expectations.

Three Months Later this Subject Came Back Around

A missionary from Estonia, Sherry Hytinen, came to speak at the Institute about three months later. As she and Dr. Frase talked about the nations and their lives, Ms. Hytinen made an unrelated comment, "I know a man who has a two year Bible school curriculum in Spanish, complete with lectures and exams." Dr. Frase interjected, "Russ Tatro?" She responded, "How do you know him?" He said, "I met him on a flight, when we were about 37,000 feet in the air. Russ Tatro offered his curriculum to me." She said, "You need to accept his offer!" She was so emphatic about her suggestion, and promised to make the call, and have it sent immediately. A few days later a package arrived. Dr. Frase briefly looked at it then set it aside, moving on to more pressing matters. Two days later he went into Cuba on a ministry trip.

LISTEN UP! THIS IS GOD AND I'M TELLING YOU ONE MORE TIME, YOU NEED THIS CIRRICULUM!

Several weeks after returning from Cuba, Dr. Frase, turned to his credenza and spotted the CD Rom of the Spanish curriculum. It was at that moment he recognized the divine provision, for what it was. He began to "connect the dots"[4] and realized that he really did need this Spanish curriculum. He deducted: Cuba speaks Spanish and they need this study to train up a generation of leaders. He called his 82-year-old Puerto Rican friend, Sam Santos. It had been Santos, who had taken him into Cuba the first time, and it was, to him he immediately turned, to share his divine provision. "I have a two year Spanish curriculum with lectures and exams. Can we use this in Cuba?" This veteran missionary began to weep, on the phone. "Oh brother Russ, I have been praying for 13 years for a Bible school for Cuba."

The Cloud Was Moving[5], and So Must Russ and Lana

The Institute was closed, and now Dr. Frase found himself heading back into Cuba, loaded with the tools to begin educating Cuban Christians with this new course work. Having set up a new ministry, by the name of: Joshua Nations, Inc., Russ, and Lana set out to establish a new vision. Within a year over 24,000 students had been enrolled, and within 9 years they had over 46,000 students in Cuba and had personally handed out 16,700 diplomas.

> I JUST LOVE LIVING UNDER THE CLOUD, WHEN MY CLOUD MOVES, SO DO I.

Soon after the initial thrust into Cuba, Dr. David Shibley, founder of Global Advance[6] invited Dr. Frase to come to speak to his staff, in Dallas, Texas, about what had developed in Cuba. Upon hearing Russ's talk, Dr. Shibley expressed his desire to introduce the Joshua

Nations Bible Training centers into the 85 nations where Global Advance was present and working.

For Dr. Frase, Cuba had become his signature nation with so many responses to his mandate to train leaders. Now it was expanding right in front of him. Just nine years later, Dr. Russ Frase has successfully seen 6,700 schools inaugurated in 44 nations, with the curriculum used in 55 different languages, and to a total of 146,401 students. They have graduated 31,300.

When the Institute closed in 2005, Russ had no idea what his next step would be. He did not see the bigger picture, but the Holy Spirit was working on his behalf laying out before him an opportunity on a grand scale requiring a higher level of creativity. He traded in his two classrooms for 6,700 schools. Russ says it this way: "It is amazing when you get the chance to live 'Life without Limits'."

Here are some quotes of people you may have read after. Perhaps you can build your own mission statement, or, as it could be called, "My commitment to living life to the full."[7]

"LOOK AT A DAY WHEN YOU ARE SUPREMELY
SATISFIED AT THE END. IT'S NOT A DAY WHEN YOU
LOUNGE AROUND DOING NOTHING; IT'S WHEN YOU'VE
HAD EVERYTHING TO DO, AND YOU'VE DONE IT."
MARGARET THATCHER

"GOOD COMMUNICATION IS AS STIMULATING AS
BLACK COFFEE AND JUST AS HARD TO SLEEP AFTER."
ANNE MORROW LINDBERG

"LIFE IS NOT MEASURED BY THE NUMBER OF BREATHS WE
TAKE BUT BY THE MOMENTS THAT TAKE OUR BREATH AWAY."
UNKNOWN

"WORK LIKE YOU DON'T NEED THE MONEY,
LOVE LIKE YOU'VE NEVER BEEN HURT, AND
DANCE LIKE NO ONE IS WATCHING."
SATCHEL PAIGE

"SUCCESS IS NOT THE RESULT OF SPONTANEOUS
COMBUSTION. YOU MUST SET YOURSELF ON FIRE.
REGGIE LEACH

"TWENTY YEARS FROM NOW YOU WILL BE MORE
DISAPPOINTED BY THE THINGS YOU DIDN'T DO THAN BY
THE ONES YOU DID DO. SO THROW OFF THE BOWLINES.
SAIL AWAY FROM THE SAFE HARBOR. CATCH THE TRADE
WINDS IN YOUR SAILS. EXPLORE. DREAM. DISCOVER."
MARK TWAIN

"IF YOUR SHIP DOESN'T COME IN, SWIM OUT TO IT!
JONATHAN WINTERS

"CHANCE IS ALWAYS POWERFUL. LET YOUR
HOOK BE ALWAYS CAST; IN THE POOL WHERE YOU
LEAST EXPECT IT, THERE WILL BE A FISH."
OVID

"EXPERIENCE IS A HARD TEACHER BECAUSE SHE
GIVES THE TEST FIRST, THE LESSON AFTERWARDS."
VERNON SANDERS LAW

"YOU DON'T STOP LAUGHING BECAUSE YOU GROW
OLD. YOU GROW OLD BECAUSE YOU STOP LAUGHING."
MICHAEL PRITCHARD

"LIFE IS A GREAT BIG CANVAS; THROW
ALL THE PAINT ON IT YOU CAN."
DANNY KAYE

"LET US SO LIVE THAT WHEN WE COME TO DIE
EVEN THE UNDERTAKER WILL BE SORRY."
MARK TWAIN

"IF YOU THINK YOU CAN, OR THINK
YOU CAN'T, YOU'RE RIGHT."
HENRY FORD

"PATIENCE HAS ITS LIMITS. TAKE IT
TOO FAR, AND IT'S COWARDICE."
GEORGE JACKSON

"YOU CAN'T TURN BACK THE CLOCK.
BUT YOU CAN WIND IT UP AGAIN."
BONNIE PRUDDEN

"A MIND IS LIKE A PARACHUTE, IT
DOESN'T WORK IF IT ISN'T OPEN."
FRANK ZAPPA

"YOU CAN'T DO ANYTHING ABOUT THE
LENGTH OF YOUR LIFE, BUT YOU CAN DO
SOMETHING ABOUT ITS WIDTH AND DEPTH."
EVAN ESAR

"ADRENALINE IS PART OF GOD'S PLAN – A GIFT
THAT SHOULD NOT BE BURIED OR NEGLECTED.
LIVE FULL, RICH, ADVENTUROUS LIVES THAT
YOUR CHILDREN WILL BE PROUD OF; AND YOU
WILL SQUEEZE THE NECTAR OUT OF LIFE!"
CAMERON BISHOP
SON OF RON & CHRISTI BISHOP

"LIFE CAN ONLY BE UNDERSTOOD BACKWARDS;
BUT IT MUST BE LIVED FORWARDS.
SOREN KIERKEGAARD

"COURAGE IS BEING SCARED TO DEATH
- BUT SADDLING UP ANYWAY."
JOHN WAYNE

Endnotes

1. This has been my mission statement for a number of years. Although this statement did not originate with me, it resonated with me. It is adapted from the mouths of a number of famous people including Richard Branson, Mavis Leyrer & Hunter S. Thompson. The objective is not to live dangerously, but to take advantage of opportunities, and not to shy away from risk, by always playing it safe.

2. Dr. Russ Frase, Joshua Nations, Inc., PO Box 745728, Arvada, Colorado 80006

3. In Memory of Russ Tatro – YouTube www.youtube.com/watch?v=kzFaqNfcGDY – Russ and Wendy Tatro founded Living Word Missions, PO Box 687, Wilmington, MA 01887. Russell Tatro (1954-2006) Russ and Wendy served with a focus on Liberia and Cameroon for nearly 30 years. He preached his last message entitled: *"The Holy Spirit"* at Teen Mania Ministries in May 2006.

4. En.wikipedia.org/wiki – In adult discourse the phrase "connect the dots" can be used as a metaphor to illustrate an ability (or inability) to associate one idea with another, to find the "big picture."

5. FACT: Throughout the wilderness, Israel moved only when the cloud moved. Numbers 9:17-22 CEV "The Lord used this cloud to tell the Israelites when to move their camp and where to set it up again. As long as the cloud covered the tent, the Israelites did not break camp. But when the cloud moved, they followed it, and wherever it stopped, they camped and stayed there, whether it was only one night, a few days, a month, or even a year. As long as the cloud remained over the tent, the Israelites stayed where they were. But when the cloud moved, so did the Israelites.

6. Global Advance, PO Box 742077, Dallas, Texas 75374-2077 USA

7. www.jamesholmes.com/quotes.html – These are all quotes from this website.

Chapter 20

A YOUNG PERSON CAN MENTOR TOO!

UNDERSTANDING, OPEN HEART, NEW PERSPECTIVES

If you were to make an international move to another nation, to China, or Africa, Bolivia or Estonia, you would need to spend some time with someone there who has the capacity to mentor you in their national and local culture. In that case, the mentor you would work with just may be one-half, or even one-third your age. Some of the things you'd glean are:

* You would benefit from knowing how their thinking is different to yours.

* How their religion impacts the culture in which they live.

* A bit about the history of their nation and why it is the way it is.

* What their language is and the uniqueness of their culture.

* How their foods are unique to those from your home country.

- How their laws are different to your laws, in everyday living, as well as on the highways.

- Are you innocent until proven guilty?[1] Or are you guilty until proven innocent?[2]

- Do the police have radar for speed detection in their cars?

- What is the possibility of them declaring "Marshall Law" anytime soon?

- Is their government stable? And how stable is their currency?

- Etc. etc. etc.

The reigning culture of your day (when you were young) certainly is different from the reigning culture of the 21st century. I hesitate to inform you, but "Happy Days are not here again."[3] I am assuming that you are still residing in your home country. If you are, then you must admit that times have changed, society and its paradigm have made adjustments and you are even finding yourself facing a changing political environment. In light of that, you would do well to seek out someone who can "speak into your life" on the subject of your changing world. Even if you find yourself holding a different opinion on issues, you will grow in your grasp of the world you live in and you will benefit by having this exchange. Keep in mind, that as a bonus, you will empower a younger person. Grandfathers like empowering younger people.

What is it like to Immigrate to a New Country?

IT FEELS GOOD TO BE BONA FIDE, NO LONGER AN ALIEN.

Let me give you an example. We have gone into Zimbabwe many times. One of our friends shared his own experience of when the Rhodesian War resulted in their declaration of independence, thereby becoming Zimbabwe.[4] He confided to us that there had been so many changes in his nation, the name, government, laws, currency, the national anthem, the flag and the passport; in the end he had to immigrate both legally and mentally to his new home, even though he was born in that land. He did not have the luxury of staying Rhodesian, but had to become Zimbabwean, thus changing legalities, loyalties and worldview. Clearly he had to get the war out of his spirit.

WHY IS THE WORLD SWIRLING AROUND ME? EVERYTHING IS SPINNING ... SOMEBODY PLEASE MAKE IT STOP.

I think his dilemma and yours may have similarities. Everything around you has moved in a new direction, which may leave you feeling like you are losing control. As a result, you need to be briefed on your new surroundings. Everything but the weather and gravity has become different, because society does not stay the same. The generations change with the changing culture, customs, and paradigms. You would do well to find someone who has the capacity to mentor you so that you remain relevant, and better able to understand what you're dealing with. You would be amazed how this younger person could actually help walk you through a clearer evaluation of what is before you. Remember, he just may be able to disarm the war that may be building in your heart, and spirit, against those you feel are the perpetrators of these changes. It may be that not all of them are your enemies, but you just need to understand the new boundaries. Of course, you cannot change everything around you, but you can soften your reactions and responses, and hopefully, be able to have a happy face and a heart full of hope for the balance of your assignments in this world. Just remember that you can never justify grumpiness and hatefulness. Write your epitaph now and state the things you wish to be remembered for, and then pledge to use it as a standard to which you will grow.

Find a Young Mentor you can Learn from who will Delight you, in the End

There is a young person out there, and it may be your grandchild, or your son, who could spend time with you, to help you grasp positives, possibilities and purpose. They will prove to be invaluable in helping you see new doors and new avenues you can walk down. God is in this because, often we find that, as we come to the last few chapters of our lives, there is need for more runway and we are about to outlive the amount of tarmac, which we'd normally have before us. You don't want to crash, and this young person may be able to awaken a new level of understanding.[5] It is second nature to him, or her, and yet so strange for you, as if you were in another culture in another part of the world.

When you ask an individual to mentor you, it must be clear what you're asking them to do for you. You are asking them to assume a role. You are asking them to hang out with a purpose. It may involve going for coffee, or at a relaxed setting. If you are married, and they are of the opposite sex, even if it is a granddaughter, then it may be an opportunity to include your wife, for example. One more thing: you are not asking them to mentor you in areas of accountability, but in the arena of the culture of the world they understand better than you. This could be a grand experiment for you and one, which will introduce some surprises as well.

One more thing, if you empower a young person to teach you, then you have complimented them in so many ways, that mere words cannot accomplish. So, take note that you may just earn the opportunity to speak into their life, as well.

Endnotes

1. www.law.cornell.edu/wex/presumption_of_innocence - *Legal Information Institute. Presumption of Innocence.* "The Presumption of Innocence is one of the most sacred principles in the American criminal justice system, holding that a defendant is innocent until proven guilty. In other words, the prosecution must prove, beyond a reasonable doubt, each essential element of the crime charged."

2. www.opensocietyfoundations.org/publications/presumption-guilt - *Presumption of Guilt: The Global Overuse of Pretrial Detention.* "Around the world, millions are effectively punished before they are tried. Legally entitled to be considered innocent and released pending trial, many accused are instead held in pretrial detention, where they are subjected to torture, exposed to life threatening disease, victimized by violence, and pressured for bribes. It is literally worse than being convicted: pretrial detainees routinely experience worse conditions than sentenced prisoners. The suicide rate among pretrial detainees is three times higher than among convicted prisoners, and ten times that of the outside community. Pretrial detention harms individuals, families, and communities; wastes state resources and human potential; and undermines the rule of law."

3. The songs of your youth are certainly not the songs of today's youth. "The Fonzie," or the "Fonze." Henry Winkler played, The Fonzie, in the US TV series "Happy Days."

4. www.sahistory.org.za/dated-event/zimbabawean-independence-day - Zimbabwe Independence Day. On April 18, 1980, Southern-Rhodesia gained independence from the British, taking the name Zimbabwe.

5. www.martynemko.com - ***When Young People Mentor Older Ones***, We normally think of older people mentoring younger ones. Yet there are good reasons for doing the opposite. As we get older, it's easy to lose track of what's the latest and greatest. If we can swallow the ego threat of being mentored by a young whippersnapper, Gen-X mentors offer a fast way to get current.

Is There a Grandfather in the House?

Chapter 21

Make Friends with Different Kinds of People

Peers, New Friends, Enlarging Borders

Nothing will ever replace the beneficial and valuable friendships, of your peers. They bring interests common to you from your past, as well as your age culture. You cannot do without these kinds of friendships as long as they are available to you. The time may come when you are one of the decreasing members of your age group and you must value them as long as you can. During times when you feel lonely or disconnected, it will be among such friends that you will usually find solace and deep laughter.

However, lots of leaders only make friends with their ministerial peers. It reminds me of the older lady who was so concerned that all of her friends had already passed. She felt concern, because she

> DON'T JUST MAKE FRIENDS THAT RESEMBLE YOU ... FIND THOSE WHO ARE FROM A DIFFERENT LINE OF WORK. THEN BE QUIET, LET THEM TALK ... WHILE YOU LEARN.

had lived so much longer, they would be of the opinion that she had missed heaven and gone to hell.

I had one friend who never made close friends with those in secular work, with whom he had little in common. He played golf with and spent vacations with those who had the same vocational and theological interests. He actually retired, uprooted and moved from his city to another state to be near another pastor friend, who did the same. Then he moaned to me that his friend stayed back in the Midwest with his family at least half of the year. He said to me these words: "Now, I am stuck alone in that city with no friends, and nobody to fellowship with." In the end, he sold his home and moved back to his original city, to live out the rest of his days.

Actually, my dear friend inspired me to make sure that I make loads of friends, both inside and outside of the church, for lots of reasons and one of them to insure that I would never get into such a predicament. My choice has been to draw a big circle and to include many people who will effectively sharpen my skills.

Even Grandfathers can have a Social Calendar

Grandfathers can become quite predictable, stuck in the mud, and inflexible. Don't be like so many grandfathers. Be like Jesus and open your arms wide to embrace all kinds of people.[1] One day Jesus was invited to the home of Matthew for a meal. Matthew was a former tax collector[2], and now one of Jesus' disciples. It is clear that Matthew did not dump all of his friends, but seemed to recognize that they were a part of those he could influence to improve their lives and hearts, even to the point of introducing them to Jesus. His new ideals had changed his own life, and he felt he could be a positive influence to them. A lot of disreputable characters came and joined them. When the Pharisees saw him keeping this kind of company, they had a fit, and lit into Jesus' followers. 'What kind of example is this from your Teacher, acting cozy with crooks and riffraff?'"[3] It even goes on to speak of just how effective Matthew had been by stating clearly that they had become followers of him.[4]

> "FRIENDSHIPS ARE VITAL FOR WELL BEING, BUT THEY TAKE TIME TO DEVELOP AND CAN'T BE ARTIFICIALLY CREATED."
>
> —ARISTOTLE

Find people in your church whom you hardly know and strike up a friendship with them. Call one of the men up, and invite him for a cup of coffee, then just talk about his work, his family and his interests, and all with no agenda. Don't conclude by inviting him to something like a men's gathering, but let him know that you just wanted to know him better. He will wonder if you are going through some kind of change on the inside. Guess what, you just may be going through some kind of change, in your road to "realness."

Let the neighbors, whom you have seldom spoken to discover that you are getting a new life and that you are more than "church." You are a whole person with a big capacity for friendships. Yes, of course, you need to win men to Christ, and you must be more a tool of witnessing for Him. And yet, you are personally in need of a remake on your style of being a tool to win men. Try making friends out of them before you pursue them, leaving yourself open to being viewed as a bounty hunter. This is a way for you to discover new ways of communicating with others. In this Post Christendom Era, we must realize that not everyone wants what you have. They need to see you as transparent and real, not super-spiritual and phoney. All of this is for your good as much as it is for the good of those around you. In short, do not reflect "agenda" in your composure.

Jesus actually said to "make friends for yourselves of unrighteous mammon."[5] How can you be a light in a dark place if you only engage in fellowship with the light? Don't allow people to put you in fear of their criticism. Go to the pub, and order Ginger Ale, Sprite or even milk[6], but don't just go to the golf course with close friends, or to the altar, or the office. Find people who need friends and make friends out of them. Broaden your circle and draw them in, for no purpose but to make friends of them. You need friends in every walk of life.[7] You need to cross paths with the Good, the Bad and the Ugly.[8] I realize that you have to guard against only having unsavory friends, as they surely can corrupt your own character.[9] But, you do not enter those friendships as a weak observer, but as a man or woman of God who has decided that too many Christians do all their fishing from the pools of other churches, rather than from the fishing hole where sinners live. Go to the "Mammon Lake" and fish for mammon who need Jesus. You will discover that sinners do make good Christians. The challenge is that, too often Christians want to cry out, "Leper, Leper," pointing out the faults of the non-Christian instead of using honey to draw them into a life of transformation.

IT REALLY IS AMAZING HOW FRIENDSHIP JUST MAY BE THE BEST "FIRST STEP" TO BROADENING THE WORLD OF THOSE YOU MEET.

Certainly, after you have shown yourself to be real to them, something about you will draw them to the Lord of your life.

How can you Win a Leper, if you Never Touch a Leper?[10]

A dear friend of mine started a ministry to lepers[11] in his area of Central India. We have been friends with Pastor Ernest P. Komanapalli[12] and his wife Rachel since our first meeting in 1971. We have stayed in their home while they lived in Rhode Island and met occasionally in various nations. Ernest visited us while we were living in Germany and we worked some together in the Republic of Central Africa, under the auspices of a fellowship of French churches, based in Grenoble, France. Ernest is a great leader and a man of noble character. He and Rachel have established quite a number of ministries, including hundreds of churches, orphanages, hospitals, Bible Schools, and even two junior colleges in the nation of India. I have always been impressed with Ernest's leadership and value their friendship.

LEPERS ARE JUST LIKE YOU, EXCEPT FOR THE BATTERED AND BRUISED EXTERIOR.

There are two occasions, which set this man of God apart with regard to the dreaded disease of leprosy. I will relate them to you as he told the first to me and the second I discovered on his website:

Ernest was visiting a colony of lepers and greeting them one afternoon. He was keeping a safe distance while trying not to look too obvious, when the Holy Spirit spoke to his heart and urged him to step forward and embrace them. His first thought was, "No, Lord,"[13] when the Holy Spirit said, "If you do not touch these lepers, you will not be accepted." He waded into the group and hugged them without fear of contagion. He realized that God was his protector.

The second story occurred in 1971, the same year we met. During a Sunday service, a group of lepers entered into the church at Amalapuram, causing a great stir among the people. People stared and were uncomfortable, not knowing what to do or how to treat the newcomers. The lepers sat through the service and then came to the altar and accepted the Lord. They came back the following week bringing more lepers who also were saved. This happened for three weeks until communion Sunday.

On the first Sunday of the month, as was the custom, a cup was passed. The cup came back to Pastor Ernest stained with the leper's marks. Ernest lifted the cup but hesitated to partake of it. At that very moment the Lord spoke to him saying, "this is the cup I drank from. Every sin was in that cup, every curse was in that cup, and every disease was in that cup including leprosy."[14] Something happened in Ernest's heart and the stained cup was no longer a cursed cup, but a blessed cup. Ernest drank from it. The Lord baptized the congregation with his love that day.

From that experience was born New Life Center, a community, and outreach for lepers. 50 families now live with dignity in the community and over 120 lepers are cared for in the leper care project. Much progress has been made to help them recover and join society again as normal human beings."[15]

How can you win a leper, if you never touch a leper? The Holy Spirit will give you wisdom to reach out and to succeed in this effort to be wise in dealing with the world around you. Jesus admitted, because he knew what was in man,[16] that "the sons of this age are shrewder and more prudent and wiser in (relation to) their own generation (to their own age and kind) than are the sons of light."[17]

"Streetwise people are smarter in this regard than law-abiding citizens."[18] So, seek out the stranger, the disenfranchised, and the foreigner and also make friends with those who drive the taxi, bake at the bakery, serve your table in your favorite restaurant, stand in line at the Post Office, and repair your automobile. Stop by the Fire House, the hospitals, or the Police station and make friends of every social economic level of society. You need their friendships as much as any others you have already amassed.

Go Out and Find Them

When we were pastoring the Village Church in Maun, Botswana[19] we made it a practice to invite the owners of the local restaurants to our home for dinner. We told them, "you cook for us frequently, and so may we prepare a meal for you in our home?" They always responded and we had great visits, and broadened our world with great conversation, plus showed them we were open for friendships. Don't do all the talking. Ask them to tell you things like, "What is the most exciting and enjoyable experience you have had in your life? What made you choose your profession?" Catch the world off guard and be better friends than the rest of their clientele. In every nation we have lived, we have consistently made this our practice, and lifestyle.[20]

HOSPITALITY: MAY WE PREPARE A MEAL FOR YOU? COME TO OUR HOME THIS TIME.

We have lived in Ireland for nearly two years and have made lots of friends in our coastal village. During this time we have frequented restaurants, coffee shops, butcheries, bakeries, pharmacies, and weekly markets. The varied personalities of the "locals" have been diverse and engaging, giving us many short moments of conversation. We decided to "give back" to these friendships by inviting them to our home for an "open house." Christmas is a good time to open your heart to your community realizing that you'll be met with a warm response. Everyone is interested in an evening out. Young people are especially in a mood to do unusual things. We also recognized that we have a lot of Eastern Europeans in our area, who do not have so many friends. We served them "sweets and savory treats," limited the invitation to from 3-8 pm and informed them they could stay as long or short of time as they wished. In our invitation we suggested that all year long they have been friends to us, and we would like to open our home to serve them for an evening. The response was excellent and now we are planning to implement other ideas in the future.

By embracing them, by making friends out of them, you will broaden your horizons and strengthen your grasp of judicial wisdom.[21] When you limit your circle of friends to a small group of predictable people with your similar worldview, you shrink and weaken your world.

So, gather up your courage, your stamina, and your biggest smile; making friends of mammon, while you have opportunity. The benefits will amaze you. When life is finished, your family will be huge. Read these prophetic words from Isaiah:

"CLEAR LOTS OF GROUND FOR YOUR TENTS! MAKE YOUR TENTS LARGE. SPREAD OUT! THINK BIG! USE PLENTY OF ROPE, DRIVE THE TENT PEGS DEEP, YOU ARE GOING TO NEED LOTS OF ELBOWROOM FOR YOUR GROWING FAMILY. YOU'RE GOING TO TAKE OVER WHOLE NATIONS,

YOU'RE GOING TO RESETTLE ABANDONED CITIES. DON'T BE AFRAID—YOU'RE NOT GOING TO BE EMBARRASSED. DON'T HOLD BACK— YOU'RE NOT GOING TO COME UP SHORT."[22]

Endnotes

1. Luke 16:1-12 NKJV Parable of the Unjust Steward – verse 9 "And I say to you, make friends for yourselves by unrighteous mammon, that when you fail, they may receive you into an everlasting home.

2. www.merriam-webster.com/dictionary/publican – A Jewish tax collector for the ancient Romans. A collector of taxes or tribute.

3. Matthew 9:10 MSG

4. Mark 2:15 KJV

5. Luke 16:9 NLV "I tell you, make friends for yourselves by using the riches of the world that are so often used in wrong ways. So when riches are a thing of the past, friends may receive you into a home that will be forever."

6. En.wikipedia.org/wiki/Barnaby_Jones – In the TV detective series of Barnaby Jones, which ran on CBS from 1973-1980, Buddy Ebsen, who played the part of Detective Barnaby Jones, was a man who abstained from alcoholic beverages. Often, on the show he would walk into a bar, in line with his work, and order from the bar, a glass of milk.

7. 1 Corinthians 15:33 NLT "Do not let anyone fool you. Bad people can make those who want to live good, become bad." – Even so, Christian people are often guilty of fishing from other churches to get converts, when sinners are the ones who need to be saved.

8. En.wikipedia.org/wiki/The_Good_the_Bad_and_the_Ugly – The 1966 Spaghetti Western movie staring Clint Eastwood. The idea is the extremes of three kinds of people in the movie; namely those who are good, those who are bad and those who are ugly. Some would agree that this is mixed up and should be the ugly, the uglier, and the ugliest. Still, in humanity we will have those crossing our paths, which are of these three different natures.

9. 1 Corinthians 15:33 NLT "Do not let anyone fool you. Bad people can make those who want to live good, become bad."

10. www.merriam-webster.com/dictionary – Persona non grata – "Personally unacceptable or unwelcome." Sometimes, in the arena of human failure, people are labelled and treated, as if they are leprous. It does not mean they have the disease of leprosy, but that people who know them put them into a place very similar to "outside of the camp." They become persona non grata and no one will go near them for fellowship, etc. However, sometimes someone needs to reach out to them so that they can be restored to wholeness and to acceptance within the community. That requires courage.

11. En.wikipedia.org/wiki/Leprosy_in_India ~ Leprosy currently affects approximately a quarter of a million people throughout the world, with majority of these cases being reported from India. Leprosy is one of the least infectious diseases mainly because nearly all of the population have natural immunity against it. Nevertheless, stigma against the disease due to its disfiguring effects causes its victims to be isolated and shunned. Leprosy is also the leading cause of permanent disability in the world and is primarily a disease of the poor.

12. www.manna7.org/history.asp ~ Dr Ernest Paul Komanapalli ~ International speaker, teacher, and leader, Founder-Chairman Emeritus of Manna Group of Ministries and its college of ministries (Manna Full Gospel Ministries, Miriam Children's Home, Rock Church Ministries, Rev. K.S.J. M. Hospitals, Arunodaya Ministries and Paramjyoti Educational Foundation). He is also the Presiding Bishop of Manna Full Gospel Churches and Rock Churches.

13. Acts 10:9-13 MSG "… Peter went out on the balcony to pray. It was about noon. Peter got hungry and started thinking about lunch. While lunch was being prepared, he fell into a trance. He saw the skies open up. Something that looked like a huge blanket lowered by ropes at its four corners settled on the ground. Every kind of animal and reptile and bird you could think of was on it. Then a voice came: "Go to it, Peter—kill and eat. Peter said, "Oh, no, Lord. I've never so much as tasted food that was not kosher."

14. www.manna7.org/history.asp ~ The cup that Jesus drank, now Ernest had to drink.

15. www.manna7.org/history.asp ~ Dr Ernest Paul Komanapalli ~ The story of touching lepers in India. It takes courage to touch a leper in any scenario, and yet, sometimes it just must be done.

16. John 2:25 KJV ~ Jesus "needed not that any should testify of man: for he knew what was in man."

17. Luke 16:8 AMP ~ Jesus said, "the sons of this age are shrewder and more prudent and wiser in (relation to) their own generation (to their own age and kind) than are the sons of light."

18. Luke 16"8 MSG ~ another way of saying it is: "Streetwise people are smarter in this regard than law-abiding citizens."

19. www.lovebotswana.org ~ Love Botswana Outreach Mission Trust. Jerry and Jana Lackey established this mission. They also founded All Nations Village Church, and a ministry to children with HIV-AIDS, a Bible School and outreaches all over southern Africa.

20. We have had legal residency in USA, Republic of South Africa, Deutschland (Germany), Botswana, the UK, and the Republic of Ireland.

21. scholarship.law.berkeley.edu ~ Master of Judicial Wisdom by: Donald P. Barrett. Under the California Law Review re: the life and judicial wisdom of California Chief Justice Roger John Traynor (1900 –1983). "This judge could see right through, and detect cant (hypocritical and sanctimonious talk, typically of a moral, religious, or political nature), hypocrisy, or pettifogging (quibbling over insignificant details). He had an innate sense that told him when a seemingly irrefragable legal argument was leading to an impossible result." A mastery of Judicial Wisdom it is a coveted gift that leaders really must have, if possible. It is a good thing to ask God for Wisdom.

22. Isaiah 54:2-3 MSG

Is There a Grandfather in the House?

Chapter 22

CHANGE SOMETHING ABOUT YOUR APPEARANCE

FLEXIBILITY, THE MIRROR, PERSONA

Have you ever felt like the face staring back at you in the mirror needs a new image?[1] Maybe you could use a sprucing up, or updating. I realize that you may be pleased at how you appear, but maybe your image could take on a new tone, to give you a lift. This is not about vanity, but more on reflecting your desire to adjust how you are viewed as a leader who is responsive and visibly open to new things. The appearance of being in a rut can be just as debilitating as actually living in a rut. If you were looking for words that describe what you do not want to be perceived as, please allow me to suggest a few:

INFLEXIBLE

UNCREATIVE

UNCHANGING

UNCHANGEABLE
UNIMAGINATIVE
UNPROGRESSIVE
OUTDATED IDEAS

Even in Business Matters, You Need to Listen to God

I have had vehicles, over the years, which I decided to sell. The first thing I'd do was to get a detail job by a professional car washing service. All I had to do was improve the appearance and I would almost reconsider the sell. One day, I wanted to sell a 3 years old Volvo, S70. I took it to the detail shop and booked it in for a detail service. They committed to wash, vacuum, shampoo the carpets, and give it a wax job. Just as I was walking out, I turned to the man who was actually doing the work and said. "Sir, I realize I do not have a For Sale sign on this car, but I want you to know it is for sale. If anyone should walk into this shop and, while looking at this car, ask you if it is for sale, please say 'Yes' and then give him my business card." About 45 minutes later the phone rang. I responded by driving over to the shop, and within two hours his wife drove away in her very beautiful "looking new" Volvo. Amazing how we have to listen to the still small voice all the time. Maybe it is time for a detail job for you.

Just consider, for a moment changing your...

* Hair style

* The way you have always worn a suit and tie; perhaps you should try dress-casual.

* If you have always worn grunge, then try wearing dress casual or maybe even a suit and tie for a change.

- Note: Whatever style you are wearing frequently, may need to be changed just because… otherwise, you are definitely in some kind of rut.

- Do something different… be courageous and do something so different that it gets your attention and others.

- Do not allow yourself to stay where you have always been.

- There is a big world out there and you may have been in a subculture a long time.

- As you walk down the street examine the view and see how many are dressed like you.

- It may be time to break out of the mold and show that you're not so predictable, go ahead and take the leap.

I am not suggesting that you sell your minivan and buy a red sports car, or grow your hair long, unbutton your shirt and hang a huge gold cross around your neck. You must be reasonable. You certainly don't want to jump off the deep end, but you just may need a little help. You must redefine yourself or you may find yourself feeling like you're in a rut.[2]

When my first grandson was born, within a few days,[3] we were driving through Maryland and I stopped at a beauty salon and instructed the young lady to cut my hair. Even though I was bald on top, I had curly hair almost to my shoulders. I walked in and asked her to cut my hair completely. I was tired of looking 80's and wanted a change, today; a major change. After she had begun, I asked her if, after she was finished, I would still be able to get a perm? She said, "Certainly." I said, "Then you don't understand what I want. I want a total re-do." She cut it

AFTER YOU CUT MY HAIR, WILL I STILL BE ABLE TO GET A PERM?

all off that day. I recognized that the 80's must go and being 1998, I was ready for a change. Then again, about 12 years later, I shaved it all off. Of course, I am not sure what the next step will be. Maybe I'll grow it back... not sure, but it has only been about four years since my first shave.

I heard a senior minister make a statement several years ago saying, "Some of you pastors have had that same hairstyle for 40 years."[4] If nothing has changed about you then it just may be time you discovered some kind of change you could make. Flexibility is vital, occasionally, at least. Most people will only see what they see, when their eyes fall on you.

So you have changed some ways about how you think, and yet, you just may benefit by changing something about what they see next time your paths cross. It really does take boldness, creativity, and courage to refashion who you appear to be.

Endnotes

1. www.google.ie/search?q=define+image - Image - the general impression that a person, organization, or product presents to the public.

2. dictionary.reference.com/browse/in+a+rut - in a rut - "In a settled or established habit or course of action, especially a boring one. This expression alludes to having a wheel stuck in a groove in the road. [Early 1800s]"

3. Cole Bishop was born to Cameron & Letha Bishop on June 17, 1997.

4. The year was 1980 and the speaker of the conference we were hosting was Pastor Leonard Fox of San Bernardino, California. The church I was pastoring was in Decatur, Georgia.

Chapter 23

LISTEN TO YOUNGER MUSICIANS

CHANGING PARADIGMS, BROADENING

Learn to listen to newer musicians. They may say more to you than you could have considered possible. Branch out beyond your personal music styles. They may be wonderful, but they also are not the only bastions of wisdom. Twenty first century young people think deeply and very often scripturally. They are also God's choice for their generation, just as you were for yours.

It is to your advantage to see and approve of today's Christian young leaders and all they bring to the table, as the musical authorities of their generation. It is clear that their musical choices, and the cultures to which they belong, are not yours. But yours was different, in many ways, to the worldview of your elders when you were young.

There is a need for a cross pollination of thoughts, that could help all of us grow to accept newer and yet still spiritually strong ideas. I mentioned earlier that, if given the chance, the young leaders of today would decorate the church differently. The same goes for the music scene, in that, they would also change the music selected in the services.

Where you came from, and the culture you enjoy, will make a major impact on your musical opinions and choices. You will, quite naturally prefer certain types and possibly abhor others. The big debate between the generations, in many churches, is whether the music style should be hymns or contemporary music.

The first thing to determine is that you really must become more committed to being a mentor, and, as a result, you would be willing to surprise the younger generation by attending a musical event with them. You need to know where these kids live. You may find their entertainment to be far outside of your box, but talking with young people may help you decide, which event to attend.

"Musical preferences are biased toward culturally familiar musical traditions."[1] Our appetites for music styles are influenced by everything from what we grew up with in our own family or church traditions, to our own musical listening experiences. Even what we heard as a small child will move us towards certain genres. An example is that, if you grew up listening to a strong Irish, or German accent, then it would sound like music to your ears, but if you grew up in Asia, then you would really have to focus to understand what the Irish or German was saying. If you are accustomed to only hearing hymns in church then a Newsboys[2], or U2[3] Concert with Bono may be, for you, a real challenge.[4]

It would be good to sit with a younger person, whom you respect and ask them to help you choose a group to listen to; then do so, with an openness to help you learn what they have to contribute to their generation. Your attending would not be to critique them, as much as it is to enlarge your scope of experience. Go ahead and ask for a copy of the lyrics; that is okay. For example, if you could go to a U2 concert, you just may be surprised at what they have to give and even the impact they have had on today's emerging churches.[5] One amazing quote, by Bono[6], for example, is this: "Religion is what you are left with, after the Holy Spirit has left the building." If you were able to watch the movie, "God's Not Dead"[7], then you would see the Newsboys in action. Groups like these are operating outside of the traditional church, and are awakening a "Post Christian"[8] generation to the reality of God in this 21st Century.

OUR FAITH IS A SINGING FAITH!

It is good to stretch beyond your usual limits. It is easy for young leaders, but necessary for all leaders, to grow into a bigger space and to think new thoughts, and to expand their worldview. To respond, to grow, to broaden, is what you must do in order to fully comprehend; and then it may be possible to mentor another generation. To be courageous enough to follow through is yet another thing. You can step up to being a grandfather, if you will forgive them for being so different and so youthful. It really is a challenge to serve your generation and to do it well, but a bonus when you serve another generation well. You did well to win the Silver, but how would you like to go for the Gold?

Here is an article I recently discovered in a newspaper, on the subject of hymns vs. contemporary music in churches today:

Dear Rev. Billy Graham:

Maybe I'm just old-fashioned, but from time to time our church's music director introduces new songs into the service, and I don't care for them. I like the old hymns and wish he'd just stick with them. Should I complain to our pastor?

Mrs. E.W.W.

Billy Graham's Answer:

I know this has been a controversial issue in many churches, and I don't pretend to have all the answers, especially since I'm not particularly musical! But we have a singing faith, and God has given us the gift of music to praise him. The Psalmist declared, "With singing lips my mouth will praise you" (Psalm 63:5).

Instead of complaining to your pastor (or anyone else), I urge you to ask God to help you be grateful for all music that points us to God, new or old. No, you may not like some of it, but others do, and God can use it in their lives to encourage them and bring them closer to Christ. Remember: The old hymns you like were once new, and someone probably didn't like them, either!

Sometimes, I'm afraid a hymn can become so familiar to us that we sing it without even thinking about the words. But this is wrong, because then our singing becomes empty and meaningless. Don't let this happen to you, but meditate on the words of the songs you sing, and even turn them into a prayer.

Your music director has probably been wise to introduce new songs slowly; completely changing everything all at once can be disruptive. Pray for him and encourage him, letting him know that you're grateful for his gifts. Yes, let him know you appreciate the old hymns, but support him also as he seeks to reach a new generation through music.[9]

I certainly do not want to belabor the point, and yet, I could not resist, but to give you this cultural rendition of the challenges facing church leaders as they do all they can to navigate between the cultures within a single church. If you don't believe it, try being the music director and listen in to his meetings with the congregational members after a weekend service. Here is a funny little story about hymns and praise songs:

An old farmer went to the city one weekend and attended the big city church. He came home and his wife asked him how it was.

"Well," said the farmer. "It was good. They did something different, however. They sang praise choruses instead of hymns."

"Praise choruses?" asked the wife. "What are those?"

"Oh, they're okay. They're sort of like hymns, only different," said the farmer.

"Well, what's the difference? Asked the wife. The farmer said:

"Well it's like this… If I were to say to you, Martha, the cows are in the corn," well that would be a hymn.

If, on the other hand, I were to say to you,

"Martha, Martha, Martha, Oh, Martha, MARTHA, MARTHA, the cows, the big cows, the brown cows, the black cows, the white cows, the COWS, COWS, COWS are in the corn, are in the corn, are in the corn, in the CORN, CORN, CORN, COOOOORRRRRNNNNN."

Then, if I were to repeat the whole thing two or three times, well that would be a praise chorus."

As luck would have it the exact same Sunday a young man, a new Christian from the city church attended the small town church. He came home and his wife asked him how it was.

"Well," said the young man, "It was good. They did something different, however. They sang hymns instead of regular songs."

Hymns?" asked the wife. "What are those?"

They're okay. They're sort of like regular songs, only different," said the young man.

Well, what's the difference?" asked the wife. The young man said: "Well it's like this… if I were to say to you, 'Martha, the cows are in the corn," well that would be a regular song.

If, on the other hand, I were to say to you,

"Oh Martha, dear Martha, hear thou my cry inclinest thine ear to the words of my mouth.

Turn thou thy whole wondrous ear by and by

To the righteous, glorious truth.

For the way of the animals who can explain

There in their heads is no shadow of sense,

Hearkenest they in God's sun or his rain,

Unless from the mild, tempting corn they are fenced.

Yea those cows in glad bovine, rebellious delight,

Have broke free their shackles, their warm pens eschewed

Then goaded by minions of darkness and night

They all my mild Chilliwack sweet corn chewed.

So look to that bright shining day by and by,

Where all foul corruptions of earth are reborn

Where no vicious animal makes my soul cry

And I no longer see those foul cows in the corn.

Then, if I were to do only verses one, three and four, and change keys on the last verse, well that would be a hymn."[10]

Endnotes

1. En.wikipedia.org/wiki ~ *Culture in music cognition*

2. En.wikipedia.org/wiki/Newsboys ~ Newsboys (sometimes stylized as newsboys) are a Christian pop rock band founded in 1985 in Mooloolaba, Queensland, Australia. They have released 16 studio albums, 6 of which have been certified gold. Currently, the bands lead vocalist is Michael Tait formerly of DC Talk

3. En.wikipedia.org/wiki/Bono ~ Rock group U2, with their lead singer, Bono. The meaning of the name "BONO" is: "All Good." "Paul David Hewson (born 10 May 1960), known by his stage name Bono, is an Irish singer-songwriter, musician, venture capitalist, businessman, and philanthropist. He is best recognized as the front man of the Dublin-based rock band U2. Bono was born and raised in Dublin, Ireland... Bono writes almost all U2 lyrics, frequently using religious, social, and political themes." It is worthy of note that Bono has a deep personal commitment to Jesus Christ, and does a good job of reflecting it in U2 lyrics.

4. En.wikipedia.org/wiki ~ *Culture in music cognition.* Where you came from, and the culture you enjoy, will make a major impact on your musical opinions and choices. You will, quite naturally prefer certain types and possibly abhor others.

5. www.wayoflife.org/database/rockgroupu2.html ~ But U2 is much more than a popular rock band. U2 has a great influence in the emerging church and the contemporary worship movement. U2's lead singer Bono is praised almost universally among contemporary and emerging Christians.

6. Bono is the lead singer of U2, based in Dublin, Ireland.

7. www.rottentomatoes.com/m/gods_not_dead ~ Present-day college freshman and devout Christian, Josh Wheaton (Shane Harper), finds his faith challenged on his first day of Philosophy class by the dogmatic and argumentative Professor Radisson (Kevin Sorbo). Radisson begins class by informing students that they will need to disavow, in writing, the existence of God on that first day, or face a failing grade.

8. www.christianitytoday.com/ct/1994/september12/4ta018.html ~ *Reaching the First Post-Christian Generation.* "They are known by many names: Generation X, post-boomers, baby busters, twenty-somethings, slackers, whiners. Perhaps "Generation X"—taken from the title of Douglas Coupland's hip 1991 novel—is the moniker of choice since it signifies an unknown variable, a generation that is still in search of its identity. But whatever one calls these 38 million young men and women born between 1963 and 1977, we cannot assume they are simply the next rounds of alienated youth. What makes them unique is that they are the first generation to grow up in a post-Christian America."

9. Readers can write to the Rev. Billy Graham at the Billy Graham Evangelistic Association, 1 Billy Graham Parkway, Charlotte, NC 28201, or call (877) 247-2426. The website for the Billy Graham Evangelistic Association is at www.billygraham.org

10. www.apuritansmind.com/the-christian-walk/a-funny-little-story-about-hymns-and-praise-songs-by-author-unknown

Chapter 24

Pick Up a "Fallen Baton" (Part 1)

"There is a Balm in Gilead"

When a Leader's Moral Failure has Disappointed Everyone

David was guilty, and sometimes, in our world, significant leaders do what King David did, so long ago. It is a sad day, an abrupt day, and one, better not to happen. But it does, in far away places involving people you do not even know. They rise to high levels of success, we respond with great respect and then they fall down, down, down. It is worse than sad; it is never a happy moment and no one feels good about the situation, not even the one who has fallen. It happens in government, in business, in churches and among friends.

What is worse is when it happens in your world, in your church and among your circle of friends. I cannot and will not attempt to address the one who has fallen, or how to help him, or her and what to say to any of their families. What I do want to look at is you; the one who must pick up the pieces and help those who face the same realities, to go forward; to live again.

You are Now the Pastor and Must Bring Healing.

Those who are known to be "the responsibles" have chosen you to face the conflict, which has arisen. Because this failure has come to light it is you who must now face the victims, the core group, the congregation, the public and hopefully not the press. Someone must address the anger, the fears and the criticism. That may be you and you are worried that you were not built for this. Conflict and confrontation are not your favorite emotions, or your choice of problems to deal with in the course of your day. My advice is that you get over the stress and the personal anguish, and recognize that this is one major assignment that you must take on, because lots of people are counting on you to be the "Pastor of healing" and to apply the "Balm of Gilead,"[1] bringing healing to the hearts of those who are having to deal with an undesirable situation.

WHEN YOU MUST LEAD OTHERS TO HEALING YOU NEED GOD'S HELP.

What is the Alternative?

The lives of those who are the wounded victims must not be allowed to go on without the healing they need. We cannot, at this time consider the question of restoring the offending party, because it is just too fresh. The bloodletting may not be over yet. It is, however, the desire of all sane people to help the ones, who have done no wrong, to be restored to hope and wellbeing. The offender has done the damage, and for now, must find his audience before God. They say "time heals all wounds," but one response came this way, "The wounds remain. In time, the mind, protecting its sanity, covers them with scar tissue and the pain lessens. But it is never gone."[2]

You are a Bridge Across the "Swamp of Despondence"

Since you have been chosen to confront the present challenges, you must come to grips with your own ability to be relevant. Now is the time to shut your door, and bow your knees to the Lord. You need help so that you will have a heart of mercy, grace, and love. You must dismiss thoughts of personal anger, criticism of the alleged offender, and plead only the case of redemption. Redemption for those who feel broken, battered, and betrayed. Your assignment is to be a bridge from good times to better times, crossing over the abyss of despair, or as John Bunyan called it in "Pilgrim's Progress," the "Swamp of Despondence."[3]

JOHN BUNYON CALLED IT RIGHT, IT IS A SWAMP OF DESPONDENCE.

It is certainly good to be a part of a team of leaders, so that broad shoulders share the challenges.

The next step for you may be to find a trusted mentor who can speak a higher level of wisdom into your life. This is not the time for a life coach, to pull out of you what you need for tools. He will serve you at another time and in different ways. Now is the time for you to find someone whose life's nature displays the essence of the "Balm of Gilead." You need someone who has healing in their nature, and can impart such peace to you; so that you can give to those who are hurting, the healing they need. You need a mentor, perhaps even a grandfather. You may find it helpful to find an older person who can, at least be an invaluable prayer partner during this time.

Caution: Do not display your own anger issues, and do not feel that you must take care of all the challenges you find. For example, you may not be the one to crusade for discipline for the party, or to judge the guilty parties. Allow others to deal with the accused. Let it go and take care of being a "Healer." Again, it is vital that you be strong in whom you are, and that you are throwing stones at no one, not even the accused. At this point in time all sins are "alleged" and it is not your place to assign blame.

One question that must be asked is why were you chosen? Is it that you were the "father figure," the grandfather of the church, the one who seemed to be the most capable to respond.

ALERT!
HERE ARE 9 BREAKTHROUGH FRUITS TO IMPROVE YOUR HEALTH:

LOVE, JOY, FORBEARANCE, KINDNESS, GOODNESS, FAITHFULNESS, GENTLENESS, AND SELF-CONTROL.

If you were thought of as the "heir apparent" then you may need to decline this assignment. If you settle these questions first, then it certainly may indicate why you are on the hot seat and not someone else. You do have an awesome challenge and it will not be easy.

The first person in the role of helping to pick up the fallen baton will likely not remain as a part of the team past the first stage. Therefore, if you have any designs on continuing as the pastor, it just may not happen. If you accept this assignment, then you need to commit to this role and possibly nothing beyond it. Your assignment is to steer the ship for a while and then to allow the Holy Spirit to take care of the future.

These are the days when the hard decisions are to be made and someone with the stomach for making those decisions just may not come out of it unscathed and popular. So, before you say, "I do," make doubly sure you are up to the challenge.

Another question remains: Are you willing to come out of this trial and into your own personal transition? If you are a leader, willing to lead without fear of reprisal, but always to do the right thing and then to redirect after the fallout is realized then this may be the reason you were chosen. Now is a good time to quote the 23rd Psalm NLT:

> THE LORD IS MY SHEPHERD; I HAVE ALL THAT I NEED
> HE LETS ME REST IN GREEN MEADOWS; HE LEADS ME
> BESIDE PEACEFUL STREAMS. HE RENEWS MY STRENGTH
> HE GUIDES ME ALONG RIGHT PATHS, BRINGING HONOR
> TO HIS NAME. EVEN WHEN I WALK THROUGH THE
> DARKEST VALLEY, I WILL NOT BE AFRAID, FOR YOU ARE
> CLOSE BESIDE ME. YOUR ROD AND YOUR STAFF PROTECT
> AND COMFORT ME. YOU PREPARE A FEAST FOR ME IN
> THE PRESENCE OF MY ENEMIES. YOU HONOR ME BY
> ANOINTING MY HEAD WITH OIL. MY CUP OVERFLOWS WITH
> BLESSINGS. SURELY YOUR GOODNESS AND UNFAILING
> LOVE WILL PURSUE ME ALL THE DAYS OF MY LIFE, AND
> I WILL LIVE IN THE HOUSE OF THE LORD FOREVER

It is a formidable responsibility to take on a challenge as a negotiator, or as the leader of the troupe to "put humpty dumpty back together again."[4]

When people's emotions run high and when they go into bereavement due to a severe disappointment in someone, then those who are the leaders have a real challenge to bring order, peace, and resolution.

Having a Good Bedside Manner is Appreciated

Following your heart will help things, but remember this: you will be better off to be short on answers and long on listening. It is hard to empathize, when you have not experienced their pain. Don't stress out, trying to convince them you "feel their pain." If you are not genuine, people will know it, so just being there for them says volumes.

One of my favorite songs to be hummed during such days is this "Old Spiritual Hymn," from "There is a Balm in Gilead." Perhaps you could go onto YouTube and listen to it now:

There is a balm in Gilead
To make the wounded whole;
There is a balm in Gilead
To heal the sin-sick soul.

Some times I feel discouraged,
And think my work's in vain,
But then the Holy Spirit
Revives my soul again.

There is a balm in Gilead
To make the wounded whole;
There is a balm in Gilead
To heal the sin-sick soul.

If you can't sing like angels,
If you can't preach like Paul,
Go home and tell your neighbor,
He died to save us all.

There is a balm in Gilead
To make the wounded whole;
There is a balm in Gilead
To heal the sin-sick soul.[5]

Endnotes

1. en.wikipedia.org/wiki/There_Is_a_Balm_in_Gilead - **_"There is a Balm in Gilead"_** - "This is a well-known traditional Black-American spiritual. The 'balm in Gilead' is a reference from the Old Testament, but the lyrics of this spiritual refer to the New Testament concept of salvation through Jesus Christ. The Balm of Gilead is interpreted as a spiritual medicine that is able to heal Israel (and sinners in general). In the Old Testament, the balm of Gilead is taken most directly from Jeremiah chapter 8 v. 22: "Is there no balm in Gilead? Is there no physician there? Why then is there no healing for the wounds of my [God's] people?"

2. www.goodreads.com/quotes/140515 - Rose Fitzgerald Kennedy (1890-1995) was the wife of Joseph Kennedy and the mother of President John F. Kennedy as well as eight other children. She differed with this quote: "Time heals all wounds."

3. Google: "The Pilgrim's Progress in Modern English" by John Bunyan

4. Knowledgenuts.com/2014/01/08/humpty-dumpty-was-not-an-egg - You might think that the main character of the classic children's nursery rhyme "Humpty Dumpty" is an egg. However, historical evidence suggests that "Humpty" was actually a cannon, set up on top of a wall, used by the Royalists during the English Civil War. During a vicious battle on June 15, 1648, the enemy, known as the Parliamentarians shot a cannonball, which hit the wall beneath of Humpty. With the wall's collapse and due to its size, the soldiers could not place it back onto the wall. It was actually a military riddle, originally. In the riddle they called the cannon, "Humpty Dumpty." In the riddle it was said, that, "all the king's horses and all the king's men failed to put him back together again." However, somewhere along the way, a cartoonist gave it the appearance of "an egg."

5. "There is a Balm in Gilead." The above words are one version of the lyrics of this old spiritual song.

Chapter 25

Pick Up a "Fallen Baton" (Part 2)

Grief, Disappointment, Fortitude

What do you do when a death has caught everyone by surprise? Churches can go on without a hitch for the longest time, but when a leader passes suddenly, it leaves a void, which is difficult to fill.

It happened to us and to our home church. It was strange to see the seat, normally occupied by our pastor, but vacant on that Sunday morning. Later a number of us, near his seat had begun to wonder why he was late to the service? Why was he not present today? Then, as the clock ticked by we looked around for a guest speaker to be in waiting, but only the church family were there. Then through a number of events during that service, with the church elders coming and going, we all were informed that he had passed, in his chair, in his office and all about three hours before the service had even begun. It was a heart condition and his death was unexpected. He was young enough, he was healthy enough, but the complications were just not seen early enough.

LOSING A CLOSE ONE TO DEATH IS A TERRIBLE LOSS. SOMETIMES ONLY THE HOLY SPIRIT COMFORTER CAN BRING YOU TO A PLACE OF PEACE.

Of course, there were more details, which do not add to this conversation. But, I give the details I've given so that you will realize that someone else has walked in your shoes. We can feel your pain as you may be experiencing the pang[1] of loss even as you read these words. No one wants to go through the dreaded experience of losing a loved one, or of a significant mentor in your life. I was on the second row, near the front of the church and was called upon by the pastor's son to step up temporarily to lead the service, until the facts could be established.

We were leaving for Africa in three days to conduct leadership conferences, but delayed our departure for a week because of the funeral. Although it was tough for us, the struggle in the hearts of our pastor's immediate family was so much worse. It has been four years and we have all healed, for the most part. God has been so good to us, as we have dealt with those things, which were never in our control in the first place. Life and death come and we must manage our grief and reach heavenward for the hand of our God and the citadel of our faith.

Give Time to Heal

Upon dealing with the first week of challenges, the Eldership made a decision not to install the pastor's son for now, but to be considerate of him, allowing him time for his own healing, thus respecting his privacy. They encouraged him to step back and deal with his broken heart as well as that of his mother and siblings. It was decided, as well, that the decision on who would assume this vacancy would be addressed at a later date.

In the case of our church, we had expectations that the son of the pastor would be seen as the heir apparent, or succeeding pastor. He was young, but qualified and well loved. He was a good man, already in ministry within the church leadership and a very good Bible teacher. Still, no one saw this coming, and least of all this young man. But, to say that this was an unexpected burden upon his shoulders is an understatement.

The eldership of the church prayed and studied the situation. We were fortunate to have a number of wise men in the wings that could give wise and Godly counsel for these matters. It was decided that it would be unwise and inconsiderate to thrust a new assignment upon the shoulders of this young man who was grieving personally.

> WHEN A MAN OF GOD DECIDES HE WILL LAY HIS OWN AMBITION ASIDE TO BECOME A MAN OF PEACE ... AND ALSO A "BRIDGE," CALM SETTLES IN AND THE STORM DIES!

Those leaders appealed to the former associate pastor, who was at that time pastoring a church in Europe. He came back to help us and served for the next two years as the lead pastor, howbeit on a temporary arrangement. It was not easy for anyone involved in these challenges. I must say that this man of God, who led our church during its time of healing, did well in leading the church through their dark valley. He has now returned to his mission field and continues investing in lives in Europe and beyond. Result: Mission Accomplished.

Who Should Assume the First Leg of this Journey?

An untimely death is the worst, because of the finality of a life, which has involved a dear leader, who now is with the Lord. These times are difficult, whether the death occurred when the set man was older, or especially if the death occurred because of an unexpected medical problem, or as an accident. Tragedy hits without warning and no one is prepared because of the shock of the moment and the thrusting of responsibility upon the shoulders of the most capable and trustworthy among "the responsibles"[2]

THE BATON TAKES LONG STRIDES AND COMPLETES THE RUN. OH, DID I FORGET TO TELL YOU, THERE WERE ALSO RUNNERS IN THIS RACE?

A question, which I asked in the previous chapter, must also be asked in this chapter. Be aware that this historical relay race has so many implications, which must be considered. Please read the chapter in this book entitled: "The Race is about the baton, not the runners." The fact is that, due to the death of the pastor, the baton had been compromised and had fallen to the ground. The competition must go on, in the bigger picture, but the witnesses observing from heaven are in suspense, for this moment, until the baton is picked up and forward movement is restored. Lives are at stake and the local vision is at risk. Time is also of essence. Read these words about the "great cloud of witnesses"[3] from the Message Bible[4]:

"DO YOU SEE WHAT THIS MEANS—ALL THESE PIONEERS WHO BLAZED THE WAY, ALL THESE VETERANS CHEERING US ON? IT MEANS WE'D BETTER GET ON WITH IT. STRIP DOWN, START RUNNING—AND NEVER QUIT! NO EXTRA SPIRITUAL FAT, NO PARASITIC SINS. KEEP YOUR EYES ON JESUS, WHO BOTH BEGAN AND FINISHED THIS RACE WE'RE IN. STUDY HOW HE DID IT. BECAUSE HE NEVER LOST SIGHT OF WHERE HE WAS HEADED—THAT EXHILARATING FINISH IN AND WITH GOD—HE COULD PUT UP WITH ANYTHING ALONG THE WAY: CROSS, SHAME, WHATEVER. AND NOW HE'S THERE, IN THE PLACE OF HONOR, RIGHT ALONGSIDE GOD. WHEN YOU FIND YOURSELVES FLAGGING IN YOUR FAITH, GO OVER THAT STORY AGAIN, ITEM BY ITEM, THAT LONG LITANY OF HOSTILITY HE PLOWED THROUGH. THAT WILL SHOOT ADRENALINE INTO YOUR SOULS!"

The assignment you have assumed has landmines and challenges you may not have considered. Do not think of this as a good future assignment for you, as you must pastor for this time with integrity, and without personal ambition or an agenda for your own advancement. You must keep your eye on the goal of strengthening this congregation and not to consider the possibilities of your own coronation. Let the future be in the hands of God and with the Eldership. If you are to assume the role as on going pastor, let that promotion come from the Lord, but do not focus on such things yourself. You have a noble cause to face and there are sober realities.

Introductions Were Made

One of the benefits of traveling a lot is that you usually have friends who have gone through similar challenges. I introduced Matthew Bell to a friend of ours in South Africa by the name of George Gourlay of Harvest Church, Umhlanga. Ian Gourlay, George's Dad, was a good friend of mine, whose passing was in much the same way as our pastor in Texas. George was eventually chosen to step up and into the position of lead pastor. The interaction between Matt and George was good for both parties. It is really a good idea to talk with someone who has had the same experiences.

Of course, in both cases, there were extenuating circumstances that could have made the end story come out differently, but in both cases all have passed the test, all have grown and the baton is on the move. The race is back on track and we continue to see the relay moving forward.

The idea is that we must all keep our eye on the baton and pray that it will not be dropped again. Surely it will be dropped, somewhere along this centuries long race, but God will have a new generation of men who have no problem with their self image… they are Bridges, strong bridges and will insure the eventual outcome.

An Unspoken Reality

The first reality is that a bridge connects two landmasses. It does not go on forever, but has a limited assignment. It starts where there has been a drop off and goes to where the land rises again. So, if you are a bridge, you begin the assignment when the baton is dropped and take it until the next runner is ready to take the baton in hand.

This work does have its exceptions, but seldom works out differently: "The first person in the role of helping to pick up the fallen baton will likely not make it past the first stage. Therefore, if you have any designs on continuing as the pastor, be warned, it just may not happen. You need to commit to this role and possibly nothing beyond it. Generally, they need a leader who steps in as a healer, and a bridge, to give safe and smooth transport from life with the previous pastor to life with the future choice.

So, your assignment is to steer the ship for a while and then to allow the Holy Spirit to take care of the future. You will likely have a time frame, to respond to. This means that you can see the beginning of the tunnel and also you already know the end of the tunnel. Dates have been settled. They may go through adjustments, but the end of the tunnel will eventually arrive. Accept it, embrace it, and go for it. There is time to be made up, as the baton must be carried swiftly onward to meet up with the next runner on deck. The eyes on you are just a formality and you must be noble, be wise, remain humble and be God's vessel of use for this time.

> YOU MAY BE THE HELMSMAN, BUT MAKE SURE THE HOLY SPIRIT IS THE NAVIGATOR.

Quoting from the previous chapter: These are the days when the hard decisions are to be made and someone with the stomach for making those decisions just may not come out of it unscathed and popular. He may still be loved, but humanity being what it is, there is always risk. So, before you say, "I do," make doubly sure you are up to the challenge. Another question remains and that is this: are you willing to come out of all of this and into your own personal transition? If you are a leader, willing to lead without fear of reprisal, but always to do the right thing and then to redirect after the fallout is realized, then this may be the reason you were chosen. It really does take courage to lead.

You Are Up to this Assignment and Will Do Well

You clearly have a history with the church, and therefore were called because of a genuine respect for your pastoral gifts and abilities. You are strong, a man of faith, and have a good "bedside manner." People feel comfortable around you and enjoy your leadership style. You were the best choice to step in, so man up and keep things going forward and to an acceptable end. I do not know you, at this reading, but must assume that you are quite the accomplished leader and well able to take this congregation into the future. That was a risk the leadership took when they called you. They did not call you to convey upon you the long-term responsibilities, but rather to ask for your help to squelch fears, comfort hearts, and address complaints, which will surely be directed toward the church leaders, any number of staff members or even the deceased pastor. The leaders have trusted you and banked on your having lots of grace. They are also confident that you'll check your ego at the door. So, chin up, get on with the job as we have a race to get back on track.

So, the Spotlight, During this Time, is on You

Your shoulders feel the weight of being the leader in the house. At first the telephones rang frequently and you were so busy. But, now, they don't ring so much and you are actively encouraging lots of people each day. Between leadership meetings and counselling times, your plate is full and you are drained at day's end. You will be challenged to keep your serotonin levels up. It may be good to go to the gym, or even take your wife out to dinner more frequently, if possible, so she does not get discouraged with all that is going on. It seems like slow moving at times, but if you will lower your own personal expectations, then you'll come out of the other end of the tunnel good to go.

OUR FEARLESS LEADER DIED, BUT JESUS IS VERY MUCH ALIVE.

Take time for your self, as you will find moments when you'll wish you had never taken on this daunting job. It often feels more like a job and less a ministry, but

210

ministry it is and, again, lives are at stake. The previous pastor was bigger than life and you are not competing with his persona, as you are a different person. But, if you steady the course it will turn out well. Just keep your bag, which is full of "the Balm of Gilead" near you at all times. The saints are hurting, hearts are tender and you are determined that not one sheep will remain wounded for long. All must experience the comforting touch of the Holy Spirit, who was sent as our comforter for such times as this. It is during such times that we realize the value of having embraced the Holy Spirit in our lives. His comfort is compelling and totally effective.

These are traumatic times for a congregation, when they knew the man, and so many felt close to the man, but he can speak to them no longer. They remember that "he gave to us his heart, he displayed to us the call in his life and now he has gone on before us to beckon us to stay the course, so that in due time, we shall follow with prepared hearts and lives for our own eternal reward."

Some People Heal More Quickly Than Others

It is amazing how different people deal with grief and distress, even when it involves a death. I am not thinking of those who are the immediate family. It is obvious that they are dealing with different issues and personal loss.

> I REALIZE YOU LOVE ALL THE PEOPLE, BUT SOME PEOPLE ARE JUST MORE LOVEABLE.

The varied people of the congregation can respond as differently as the East is from the West. Although all may have loved the Pastor or love those in leadership sincerely, the fact remains that some mourn for weeks and even months, while others seem to move on within days. It is also surprising to discover the numbers of people within the congregation who are previous leaders, or at least cousins of leaders who have good, and often not so good, perspectives. Some will graciously make suggestions, while others give out their ideas with strings attached, some even making suggestions that they will leave the church, if their suggestions are not followed.

In such cases, allow the voice of the Holy Spirit to speak to you these words, "Let them go!" You must not yield to extortion or a shake down. These people have a clear agenda and when the dust settles, their advice was suspect and serves as a warning.

You May Feel That You are Strapped to the "Bulls-Eye"[5]

It really is a sacred trust to be the man designated to lead during such times. The sacred trust is to the baton and the furtherance of the race, and at the same time to remain impartial and objective, even to your own exclusion.

We need wise men that have no agendas, and no ulterior motive. Oh, for men who have been loving fathers, but now are able to change postures and become unassuming grandfathers in the house.

You Can be a Grandfather Before Your Time

I have written this book about grandfathers. However, you must understand that it is not about your age; it is about your heart and how capable you are to meet challenges in a selfish world. There is work to be done and someone must do it, but if no one has the heart for those God given assignments then failure is imminent.

Did you know that you could find yourself flowing with the anointing of a "grandfather," even before your time, if you are able to live without selfish agendas and expectations? But you must unplug from your ego, and become the "man of transcendence," which is so needed during such times.

HOW IS YOUR IQ? DID YOU KNOW THAT YOU CAN HAVE A HIGH IQ, BUT BE TOTALLY LACKING IN WISDOM?

Older men are not the only ones gifted to respond in the ways I have described. Occasionally I meet younger men who are able to let the Holy Spirit come into their hearts on such levels that they can serve in this capacity, during times of tragedy. These young men are mature, have a solid grasp of good common sense and a sure grasp of judicial wisdom.

You can only do this if you "Think Eternal."[6] If you think temporal or fleshly then you will disappoint the "great cloud of witnesses."

The Clouds are Full of Witnesses, Cheering You On

That great "cloud of witnesses" is watching from the balcony of heaven to see if integrity and humility still remain in the church in this 21st century. Is it possible that you could be such a man?

I honestly believe that the Holy Spirit is moving and searching all over the earth for such men. Men who can step up to the plate and always do the right thing, always have the heart of a father, but not make the demands of the opportunist.[7]

It is easy to hungrily search for your next opportunity or open door, but step back and allow the Holy Spirit to guide you. He has, for you, a strong life plan, if you have deep-seated principles that are guided by depth of character. You must wait on God to bring you to assignments that will impact lives you have never met. It is a good thing to sow into the lives of strangers. That is what mission work is all about.

Suggestions of a good book: Go to Amazon.com and locate an amazing novel by Randy Alcorn called, "Safely Home." Alcorn gives lots of the proceeds of this book to support the "underground church" in China. I enjoyed reading this novel and recommend it to help you understand more about heaven and hell and everything in between. This book will brand your brain and help you relate to this subject of integrity, in ways that will surprise you. "It takes place in present-day China, and follows the story of two Harvard roommates, one American and one Chinese, who reunite decades after they graduate. The novel won the Gold Medallion Book Award for evangelical literature."[8]

Concluding Details on Our Home Church

Our home church is growing and strong. Even though we no longer live in San Antonio, Texas, we still maintain Destiny Church as our home church. Pastor Matthew Bell is the lead pastor and the church is doing well. With his Dad[9] passing, it was most difficult for all concerned. David Bell had been an inspiration as our pastor and a fantastic musician as well. Doug Pitman came in for a time and served the church, leading the congregation through a difficult patch in their history. The church, which is 75 years old, has continued to grow and has become strong under Matt's capable leadership, working also with a dynamic Eldership team.

I have to say this finally: Even though Dave's death, through no fault of his own, caused the baton to fall to the ground, Doug did a great job of picking it up, then willingly served as a "bridge" for the people of our congregation to pass from the past to the future, with minimal disruption. When Doug picked up the fallen baton, and then successfully passed it off to Matt, I really believe that Dave Bell, the accomplished musician and worship leader who served God from his keyboard, stood up and led the "great cloud of witnesses" in one deafening cheer that "the baton had not lingered, nor laid long upon the ground" and all is well, once again, for the Kingdom of God in our corner of the world. The church remains strong in San Antonio and we, for one family, are proud of the hometown team.

"Go Destiny Church"

"Go Doug Pitman"

"Go Matthew Bell"

"Go Jodi Bell" (David Bell's widow)

… And "Go Baton."

Take note that, all of this can be heard from the balcony of heaven as the "great cloud of witnesses" cheers the game onward.

Endnotes

1. www.merriam-webster.com/dictionary/pang - Pang - "a sudden, strong feeling of physical or emotional pain; sharp attack of mental anguish"

2. The French actually do have a Minister of Culture in Paris who is responsible to fashion what comes into and is used by French speaking citizens. The French Churches use this term to refer to those who are "the responsibles" in a church. In English we usually hear it referred to as "those in leadership." "The Responsibles" does have a good ring to it. These are those in leadership who are actually "the Responsibles." The buck stops with them.

3. Hebrews 12:1 NKJV "Therefore we also, since we are surrounded by so great a cloud of witnesses, let us lay aside every weight, and the sin which so easily ensnares us, and let us run with endurance the race that is set before us."

4. Hebrews 12:1-3 MSG

5. www.merriam-webster.com/dictionary/bull's-eye - Bull's-Eye - the small circle at the center of a target toward which people throw darts or shoot arrows or bullets.

6. THINK ETERNAL - This is an inspiration from a friend of mine, Gary Pokorney, former missionary to the people of South Korea. He became well known in one group of churches for always ending a conversation with these words: "THINK ETERNAL."

7. Ezekiel 9:4 CEV "Walk through the city of Jerusalem and mark the forehead of anyone who is truly upset and sad about the disgusting things that are being done here."

8. en.wikipedia.org/wiki/Safely_Home - I enjoyed reading this novel and recommend it to help you know more about heaven and hell and everything in between.

9. David Michael Bell pastored Destiny Church in San Antonio, Texas. Doug Pitman was the interim pastor. In practical terms, Doug served Destiny Church as a "bridge" from the PAST to the FUTURE. This made the transition much easier for all of us. The Lead Pastor is now Matthew Bell.

Chapter 26

Young Men Need Older Men in Their Lives!

Head knowledge is not enough ... Go for the heart too.

Aquestion for young men: Have you thought about the advantages of being mentored by a grandfather? I realize that there are some cynics who put grandfathers in the category of old. It has been said that one of the characteristics of the 21st century is that old is out and young is in. There is another famous quote, "Those who do not learn from history are destined to repeat it."[1]

Let me remind you that an apprenticeship, studying with one of the greats gives you a valuable advantage. Some characteristics of those who mentor is that they have "fought a good fight" and have already run a long race.[2] They are at a place in their lives that they want to share with someone what they have learned. They need to pass on the oral history and personal lessons. They have mellowed a bit and no longer want to stress out, or fight, as their testosterone has diminished and their

SOMETIMES THE "MORAL COMPASS" AND THE "TRUE NORTH" NEED TWEAKING ... GRANDFATHERS ARE GOOD TWEAKERS.

appetite for war has taken leave. You will find they are happy to impart whatever wisdom they have, and all for free. They are complimented when a young hungry soul wants to listen to what they have to give. Grandfathers have built a network of friends, and have the gift of alerting you to pitfalls and potholes you will surely face along the way. They have no agenda, as they have been purified by the refiner's fire throughout the years.

Young men need to have an older man in their lives. They need him as a mentor, counselor, sounding board, and one to whom they can become accountable. I have had six fathers[3] in the Lord, who became men of significance to me. Each of these men gave me unique things. They introduced me to realms of wisdom unique to any others. I have had minor mentors as well, who gave me value, but these six were men who made significant deposits of their time. I remain grateful to them for all they gave me. They were not perfect, or all wise, but they were accomplished in their fields, respected within their communities and loved me enough to take time to invest in whom they hoped I would become.[4]

This talk is not about gathering up a load of sons for grandfathers to mentor. However, as much as it is a benefit for a young leader to be mentored, it is also a blessing for older men when they are invited to speak into the lives of younger men. This may serve as a wake up call, so that older men do not think their assignments are finished.

Young man, it is best you come to him, rather than expect him to run after you. Remember, he doesn't do well as a "runner," and you're the one who will benefit most by the input of a mentor. Today you may not see all the value of his wit and wisdom, but the day will come when he is gone and you will be grateful for what you learned from him and will find yourself quoting him frequently. You will see his wisdom played out for you in the arena of life, as he is gone and you continue to live out his dream vicariously in you.

There is an added advantage, in that you will be certified by whom you sat under, as Joshua was mentored by serving with Moses,[5] Elisha learned by observing the anointing on the life of Elijah,[6] Saul of Tarsus sat under Gamaliel,[7] or Timothy, who was Paul's son in the Gospel.[8] Each of these younger men realigned their personal identity and set on-track whom they would become, as they launched down the path of their own lives.

What is the Difference Between Coaching and Mentoring?

We all benefit greatly by having teachers in our lives. Those teachers, who are espousing a Biblical value system will help individuals to keep their lives accountable, disciplined and on track. One of the disciplines, which will help both in and outside of the church, in and outside of the workplace and in and outside of career choices is that of Life Coaches.

Coaches "Pull Out" and Identify Your Inner Tools

A life coach is a teacher and assumes the relationship of an instructor. A life coach pulls out what is hidden within the individual who is there for counsel.

Coaches give clarity when indecision and fear are preventing progress in a life. A coach can simplify and encourage an individual on what choices are necessary and why. The clarity they bring to those who meet with them regularly can become invaluable and encouraging. Hope can often come to a life, when a stalemate of indecisiveness seems to prevent growth.

Those who carefully select a life coach to speak into their lives should benefit greatly. Life coaches are often masters at "pulling out" the tools or talents, which are already resident within your personal makeup. The idea is that you have great talents, strong opportunities, and almost boundless energy. The challenge is that often there is a lack of clarity or understanding on how to identify your own strong points, and what to do with those talents, once they're identified. If you could only find wise counsel, and the understanding on how to evaluate your own abilities, then you could do everything so much better. This is where a life coach could be a great help.

A LIFE COACH MAY HELP YOU ORDER YOUR SKILLS AND GIFTS.

Mentors "Pour In" the Ingredients Needed For Life

A mentor is a leader and assumes the role of a father; pouring in what is needed to lubricate, enlighten and affirm an individual. Mentors pour in the ingredients needed for life and its challenges. If an individual wishes to join the ranks of leaders in any field, he will benefit greatly by seeking out a strong mentor. Those who are in a state of developing and wish to grow will find the path more clearly paved by a mentor, like Elijah, Gamaliel,

Nicodemus, or Paul. Of course the mentors available to you will not be so famous or renowned. They may have names like Tom, Pete, Liam, Sam, Jack, Sebastian, Carlos, Nigel, Neville, or Amos, and so you have to see them with the value they can give, based on the wisdom you have picked up from them in the past. But, do not be disappointed. Any of these men will bless you with wisdom beyond your present level.

Mentors will help identify how to improve your "true north" and your "moral compass."

Choosing Between a Life Coach and a Mentor

When choosing what kind of input could best benefit you in your "growth challenge," you must ask what the desired end results are to be? What are the life changing goals you wish to pursue? If you wish to grow into a leadership position—whether in ministry, or in business—then ultimately a mentor will do you a great service, because he will help boost your confidence level.

A LIFE COACH "PULLS OUT" WHAT IS ALREADY INSIDE OF YOU! A MENTOR "POURS IN" WHAT YOU NEED!

A life coach is a great choice, especially when it comes to job related conundrums, breaking out of paradigms and building self-esteem. Very often life itself and personal disappointments have hemmed in an individual. If only someone could help give guidance and instruction, then hope would be realized. It is a fact that even those who appear to have "all their ducks lined up" may, on occasion, come to a place where they need a life coach to shake things up and to help them think outside of the box. The life coach may be able to help you break out of your cycle, reorder your rhythm, and breathe differently.

If, however, the individual has mastered self-control, personal disciplines, and forward movement in most areas, then a mentor may be just what is needed. Even so, you may need the Holy Spirit to help you decide which is needed, and who could give you the best challenge. If there is a desire to rise to a higher level of achievement in ministry, for example, or even in a secular line of work, a personal mentor may boost the confidence level and show the path to growth more clearly. Much of what a mentor achieves is in areas of commitment, goals and character issues of the heart.

Consider that a mentor will help you with character issues or leadership challenges, while a life coach can aid you in clarifying techniques. Both are quite valuable and most of us need to go see the good doctor to get an occasional adjustment or mild tweaking.

It is a fact that everyone should benefit from time spent with a mentor. Some cultures, or the people of a variety of nations, however, have experienced a "father wound," which has been forced upon them by abusive national leaders or governmental officers. This leaves the general populace struggling for survival and often with a dysfunctional worldview; thus complicating the lives of its people. Some have even been forced to become refugees, or at least have become economically displaced or even stateless exiles. Many of these folks feel out of place and have put their guard up. Consequently, they may find it difficult to receive from any authority figure; their wounds and disappointments have left them with fears that they will fail to succeed in their new environment. As a result, they struggle with societies' expectations and their ability to get ahead. Like so many of us, they need the tender loving care, and healing nature of a good leader who can pour the Balm of Gilead into their wounds. If this is successful, they will adapt to their surroundings, will be accepted and will become a contributing part of society.

In that case, those individuals could consider asking a life coach to help them become flexible, open to change and receptive to inner sensitivity to the Holy Spirit; realizing that the ultimate teacher is the Holy Spirit. Until that person is willing to submit to the inner dealings of the Lord, then they may have to take "Baby Steps" to start on their journey. In such cases seeking out a life coach will have a good feel to it.

A grandfather is a "father" and will respond to your need to be nurtured, healed, repaired, challenged, and motivated to make the right choices and then follow through to do the right thing. He will be willing to talk about any subject you find necessary to address.

Of course there are landmines and leprous subjects, but this mentor or coach is prepared, as a lifelong learner, to help you become all you need to be in the transitions you face along the way. Grandfathers will often start your visits with prayer, and end in prayer, as the Holy Spirit must guide you both.

Endnotes

1. A variation of a quote from George Santayana (1863-1952)

2. II Timothy 4:7 Paul speaking to, Timothy, his son in the Gospel

3. 1 Corinthians 4:15 KJV ~ "For though ye have ten thousand instructors in Christ, yet have ye not many fathers: for in Christ Jesus I have begotten you through the gospel."

4. *The Joseph Story*, by Ron A. Bishop, ©2010. Dedicated to these six men.

5. Deuteronomy 31:7 KJV "And **Moses** called unto **Joshua**, and said unto him in the sight of all Israel, 'Be strong and of a good courage: for thou must go with this people unto the land which the Lord hath sworn unto their fathers to give them; and thou shalt cause them to inherit it.'"

6. 2 Kings 2:15 NASB "Now when the sons of the prophets who were at Jericho opposite him saw him, they said, 'The spirit of Elijah rests on Elisha.' And they came to meet him and bowed themselves to the ground before him."

7. Acts 22:3 TLB "I am a Jew," he said, "born in Tarsus, a city in Cilicia, but educated here in Jerusalem under Gamaliel, at whose feet I learned to follow our Jewish laws and customs very carefully. I became very anxious to honor God in everything I did, just as you have tried to do today."

8. 2 Timothy 1:1-2 MSG "I, Paul, am on special assignment for Christ, carrying out God's plan laid out in the Message of Life by Jesus. I write this to you, Timothy, the son I love so much. All the best from our God and Christ be yours!"

Chapter 27

THE AHITHOPHEL STORY

FOR SOMEONE WHO HAD ALWAYS DONE IT RIGHT, HE SURE DID IT WRONG THIS TIME!

Ahithophel was a family man, and an exemplary grandfather. He only had one son, who only had one daughter. He loved his son and was proud of him, especially because he was one of David's distinguished mighty men. Ahithophel was a high-ranking official of Israel's government. He and the king enjoyed mutual respect. This man, Ahithophel was a very wise man and one to whom the King could easily come for counsel, which was always spot on; actually, it has been said, that, to receive counsel of Ahithophel was "the same as to receive it straight from the mouth of God." Divine inspiration seemed to come to this man quite naturally. It actually could be said that, there was no man wiser in all the land than this man. Later Israel would have another king, by the name of Solomon, and men everywhere would declare him to be the "wisest man who ever lived," while also alluding that there might never be a wiser man than this King Solomon. But that would be after Ahithophel has passed, so, during his days, there was no wiser man than this man, the Secretary of State[1] of Israel by the name of Ahithophel. It came to be accepted fact that the "counsel that Ahithophel gave, in those days was treated as if God himself[2] had spoken."[3] To discover the full backstory, read II Samuel 11-17.

Ahithophel was a very dear and trusted friend to his King. Apparently, Ahithophel and David had been dear and close friends for a long time, but that friendship ended. All that had occurred in private became clear to the public and especially to the family of this high-ranking public figure. This was a national scandal.

David's Sin with Bathsheba had Far Reaching Consequences

Two of David's mighty men were directly affected by David's sin with Bathsheba. Firstly, it affected Uriah, who was her husband. When Bathsheba became pregnant, David ordered Joab to release Uriah to come home to Jerusalem. The King was unsuccessful in persuading Uriah to take some time off and sleep with Bathsheba. He then sent Uriah back to the battlefront with a secret note to Joab to assign him to the most vulnerable place in the battle, and then withdraw the backup troops, so that he would be slain.[4]

URIAH WAS FAULTLESS AND DEVOUT ... A MAN COMMITTED TO HIS KING AND HIS COUNTRY.

Secondly, it affected Bathsheba's own father, Eliam,[5] who was also one of David's loyal Mighty Men. As families go, David's betrayal and sin was expanding to the extended family. Note that Eliam only had one child, and that was Bathsheba.

Thirdly, it affected her grandfather, Ahithophel, the Secretary of State, and Eliam's father. He was highly offended and overwhelmed when the news came out that the King had committed such indiscretions as to betray the trust of Ahithophel and his family.

"You're the Man," is Not Always a Compliment

God was severely displeased with what David had done, and sent Nathan, His prophet to set the record straight.[6] The words of Nathan the Prophet may not have reached the general public, but they were common knowledge to those who made up the palace officials and staff. When the prophet made his visit and then his pronouncement, the news swept the halls and homes of everyone in close proximity to the palace as well as all the families of those in politics.

How the Story was Repeated Throughout the Realm

The Lord sent Nathan to David. Nathan said to him, "There were two men in the same city—one rich, the other poor. The rich man had huge flocks of sheep, and herds of cattle. The poor man had nothing but one little female lamb, which he had bought and raised. It grew up with him and his children as a member of the family. It ate off his plate and drank from his cup and slept on his bed. It was like a daughter to him.

"One day a traveler dropped in on the rich man. He was too stingy to take an animal from his own herds or flocks to make a meal for his visitor, so he took the poor man's lamb and prepared a meal to set before his guest."

David exploded in anger. "As surely as God lives," he said to Nathan, "the man who did this ought to be lynched! He must repay for the lamb four times over for his crime and his stinginess!"[7]

Nathan, the powerful man of God and prophet, did not hesitate but pointed his finger directly into the face of the king and declared with a powerful and forceful commanding voice, "You are the man, David, you are the man."

One Ewe Lamb ~ One Innocent Lamb

This story told to David by Nathan was even more complex than you may think. There were at least three offended parties in this story: Uriah, Eliam, and Ahithophel, as well as the wives and mothers, whose names are not given.

BATHSHEBA WAS NOT JUST A NEIGHBOR LADY, BUT THE TREASURE OF ANOTHER MAN.

Uriah was offended, even to the loss of his own life. He was the closest one to the "one ewe lamb," because, as we see in the story, Bathsheba was the "one little female lamb" and she was his beloved.

Eliam was the father of Bathsheba. Although nothing is said regarding the offence taken by Eliam in this tragedy, it must be stated that Eliam was a victim in this story. He was one of David's mighty men, and was the father of the "one ewe lamb."

Ahithophel was the father of one child, his son named Eliam, but also grandfather of the girl whom King David had lusted after and with whom he had committed adultery.

Who was "The Traveler"?[8]

David had not shown a deviant side to his nature before his encounter with Bathsheba. He did, unfortunately let down his guard, and failed morally on this occasion. This was the case of an alien thought, or a temptation, which came to David when he was not on top of the mountain, spiritually. There was every confidence in the character of the 'Sweet Psalmist of Israel," that he would not do anything like he did on this day, but the fact was that he failed, he sinned and he would face the consequences in significant ways.

So, this "traveler"[9] represents a situation, a circumstance, a temptation, a lustful thought, a stranger, and a renegade idea, which should be cast aside; but David failed to deal with it appropriately. He paid dearly, as a result. It is interesting how Nathan did not portray the traveler as a guest, or as a friend from afar, but rather a traveler; as if a "fleeting or passing through the neighborhood traveler." It was an invasive and besetting thought, as if a thief, or spirit of lust, may come into anyone's mind, but must be cast aside responsibly.

> BLAME CANNOT BE LAID AT BATHSHEBA'S DOOR. DAVID MUST TAKE IT ALL.

David should have turned his head and not looked at Bathsheba. Instead he accommodated his idle time, at a time when a king normally goes out to war with his army; by glaring too much, and for too long at the forbidden fruit, of another man's house. For this David would live to regret it.

The traveler was a negotiator who did not point out to his host that he really did not need to go after Bathsheba, as he already had plenty of women in his own household. It is likely that the women in David's world were just as pretty, just as accommodating as was needed for his desires, but it was never really about beauty, but about the moment, and about the score. David was wrong and this traveler, in the story of Nathan, was well up to the challenge to defeat its willing participant.

This traveler was a seasoned mediator, always trumpeting his own cause, and never looking out for righteousness or integrity. This traveler had an evil agenda and would not let go, once he saw a willing participant. David took in the view from his rooftop to the rooftop of the house below. She was oblivious of David's gaze and took care of her daily bath, innocent of what was about to transpire. David was violating the sacred trust between a husband and wife. Bathsheba would be drawn into a difficult and unexpected drama. Because of his high state as king, contrasted against her low state as a woman, this granddaughter of Ahithophel had few options. David was bigger than life and this became a key ingredient in what transpired on that day.

How Did this Grandfather Fail the Test?

Ahithophel grew bitter, angry and vindictive. We know this because he told Absalom that he would kill David himself, with a sword, and he counselled Absalom to violate ten of David's concubines, in public view. This was revenge, pure and simple, when you consider that he was so angry with David for having "violated" his granddaughter. He was really angry at what David had done, and it was showing through. He allowed belligerence and hatred for the king to rise up within. Of course, in a real world of carnal living, he had every right to become angry with the king, for what he had done to Bathsheba. Of course, he could not let it go, any sane grandfather would have felt no differently. Except for one thing: there is a downside to bitterness. It will affect every aspect of your life, not to mention how it will seldom lead to resolution. In the end, hatred, bitterness and vindictiveness will bring death, and so it did in the case of Ahithophel. Yes, David had done him wrong, but Ahithophel took personal vengeance on David.[10]

Is this what Justifiable Homicide Feels Like?

It is a really tough thing to deal with anger, when you feel so clearly defiled, abused and troubled by an offence committed and so close to home, by so close a friend. Ahithophel was so angry he wanted to march right down to the royal palace and commit murder. This man, the king, had shared family times with Ahithophel and

GUILTY OF MURDER BEFORE THE BULLET EVEN LEFT THE CHAMBER.

his wife, as well as with Eliam and Uriah, both of whom were among David's personal bodyguard and mighty men for years. What hurt the most was the mere fact that he could remember times when his little girl, Bathsheba, his precious granddaughter had played with her toys in the house even when David would come by for a visit. Bathsheba had grown up and into a beautiful young lady, and even had felt so honored when the King accepted Uriah's invitation to attend their wedding. No they had not spent so much personal time socializing with the King, but there she had been before the king all the days of her young life, and yet, he somehow had not seen her as his innocent neighbor and the precious loved one of his dear friends. This was too much for this grandfather, and Ahithophel wanted to do terrible things to him. Although he had felt so close to his king over the years, now he wanted to be far away from him, because he was so angry. It took days and weeks before Ahithophel could even look in the direction of the palace. He felt maligned, hostile, hateful, belligerent, noxious and even nauseated.

How would this prominent official of the Kingdom of Israel handle his job, his responsibility and close proximity to the man whom he had loved, but now loathed? These were real issues in the heart of this man, Ahithophel. How would it play out? How would he feel the first time he faced the man whom he had trusted? Could he give David advice, if he asked for it, and how could Ahithophel dance around the issue of David's offensive act against him; no not just against Bathsheba, but also against every one and every thing he had ever stood for?

Ahithophel had lived a lifetime of passing the test and making the right decisions. Wisdom had been his forte, but when the dragon struck in his life he had, for too long, forgotten to be on guard. He took for granted that he was above failure. He was not susceptible to such things as doubt, fear and all the things that come with pride. But, apparently, pride had taken root and all without his recognizing it.

This story must not be downplayed, but must be seen for what it was in the life of Ahithophel and his family. It was a human tragedy. It is easy to pick out a verse, or a chapter in this developing drama and sermonize on it, or develop ideas about it, but this was a tragedy and would go down in history as one of the greatest offenses against the heart and soul of families, if not very friends.

The big question remains: how is a man to deal with a trial like this when he feels so personally troubled by the details? Is it possible to forgive? Is it possible to look into the eyes of a man who has been your trusted confidant and comrade for so long, and let things be as they were? These are not trivial issues, but deeply troubling matters that require serious prayer and soul searching. Only God can answer the cry that dwells deep within, because there is no human counsel for times like these. Someone who has never suffered such things can make an attempt to say they understand, but only one who has heard of mercy and grace, and that straight from the very heart of God can begin to grapple with this level of betrayal.

A Man's Faith Must Remain Strong During Times of Duress

Ahithophel could have turned to God. He could have sought the comfort that only his Creator could have given, but that just did not seem to come to mind for him. If he had learned what David had learned, but presently was not implementing? If Ahithophel had remembered that God was not just some "God of convenience" or cute ornament in the national persona, then perhaps he could have gone to the temple and fallen on his face to seek help from above. But no, the pain was too deep for him and he felt he had to deal with matters in his own way. As a result he did not turn to God for help. Instead of turning upward, he turned inward. He was mistaken about the right response, and deceived himself by looking for wisdom from within his own mind. This was a big mistake and would result in sure and absolute destruction for he and all that he had stood for all of his life.

Only God Can Repair the Totally Broken Life

When trauma, troubles, vexation, and exasperation of this magnitude come your way, do not turn your search within, but turn your search to the throne of your God. Only God can calm the storm and squelch your anger. Only the Holy Spirit can stop the bloodletting.

If Ahithophel had only realized that God was there for him, then perhaps he could have seen that God can redeem even a very toxic situation. Nothing that Ahithophel could have done in his own strength would have disarmed the anger, which he felt at that moment. But, God can heal, and God can redeem and God can restore that, which seems un-restorable.

"X-Ray the soul of the vengeful and behold the tumor of bitterness: black, menacing, and malignant, perhaps even with Carcinoma of the spirit. It's fatal fibres creep around the edge of the heart and ravage it. Yesterday you can't alter, but your reaction to yesterday you can. The past you cannot change, but your response to your past you can."[11]

How Did God Redeem a Bad Situation in this Story?

If you read the rest of the story, you'll see that Ahithophel failed to see the larger picture.

The child born to the tryst between David and Bathsheba died. However, despite a wrong beginning, Bathsheba became the mother of Solomon, and life continued. The human nature is capable of rebounding and rebuilding, with the help of the Holy Spirit. The repair of human emotions, which is beyond the reach of human beings, becomes possible only, when God intervenes.

It is apparent that David took to heart the powerful words of Nathan, the prophet. He repented for all that he had done and became a committed protector of "the one ewe lamb," namely, Bathsheba. She became a very significant part of the balance of David's life and rule as king. Her son, their second child, became the designated king to replace David on the throne.

If Ahithophel had lived a long life he would have seen his great grandson become the next King, and he could have given counsel to the "wisest man who ever lived." Now that would have been a good epitaph on his tombstone.

Here is how the family line went in the future story:

- Ahithophel was the father of Eliam
- Eliam[12] was the father of Bathsheba
- Bathsheba was the mother of Solomon

So, the Golden Era of Israel's History goes like this:

- Israel's first king was Saul who reigned 40 years
- Israel's second king was David who reigned 40 years
- Israel's third king was Solomon who reigned 40 years

One Major Characteristic of Redemption is Patience

One of the principles of Redemption is that when given the chance, God can make something good out of a bad situation. If you back away from the determination to invoke vengeance, leaving that to the Lord; He will bring everything full circle and will redeem you in every way.

You can only see so far, and never around the corner. If the past is prior to your birth, then you will be short on details, and likewise, because the future is around the corner, then you will be unable to judge it wisely. Since it is a given that you cannot possibly see the "larger picture," then leave lots more to God, since He does have clarity on such things. Be patient and yielding so that God can freely sort your challenges out. If you take vengeance into your own hand, then you are, effectively, tying God's hands, preventing the Balm of Gilead from being applied. Remain aware that you may not live long enough to see the redemption with you own eyes; but stay confident that God will complete every thing He takes on for you. He is in the business of healing, bringing hope, and restoring everything that gets too broken for man to deal with. God has a long track record of applying redemption to bad situations.

Here are three quotes on patience to consider:

NEVER CUT A TREE DOWN IN THE WINTERTIME.
NEVER MAKE A NEGATIVE DECISION IN THE LOW TIME.
NEVER MAKE YOUR MOST IMPORTANT DECISIONS WHEN
YOU ARE IN YOUR WORST MOODS. WAIT. BE PATIENT.
THE STORM WILL PASS. THE SPRING WILL COME.
ROBERT H. SCHULLER

PATIENCE IS NOT SIMPLY THE ABILITY TO WAIT
– IT'S HOW WE BEHAVE WHILE WE'RE WAITING.
JOYCE MEYER

SOMETIMES THINGS AREN'T CLEAR RIGHT AWAY.
THAT'S WHERE YOU NEED TO BE PATIENT AND
PERSEVERE AND SEE WHERE THINGS LEAD.
MARY PIERCE

Seniority Will Not Exempt You, When it Comes to Failure!

No matter how wise or how old you are, you can make very bad, or wrong decisions when facing a crisis, if you fail to remember the Bible principle, "vengeance is mine, says the Lord, I will repay."[13] Toxicity is a condition, which can defeat and annihilate the reputation and good name of even the wisest individuals. There is no seniority in the Kingdom of God. Foolish practices can reach all the way back from the grave to embarrass and destroy a legacy.

Avoid picking up an offense by anyone. Remember, the closer the offender is to you, the worse it will hurt. It is imperative that you keep in mind that God remains in control of your destiny. Sometimes we get the idea that what someone else does will derail God's plan of purpose and provision in our lives. During such times, if you take your eyes off of Jesus, you will sink into a mire of self-pity, thus inviting toxicity into your realm. The best advice is to cast off the destroyer and embrace the healer. You must pick up a bag of the balm of Gilead and have faith in God that He will sort things out for you. Now is the time to commit to the healing process. Let it go. Selah!

FOOLISH PRACTICES CAN REACH ALL THE WAY BACK FROM THE GRAVE TO EMBARRASS AND DESTROY A LEGACY.

Ahithophel had neither expectations of redemption, nor patience for it. He kicked into gear and changed sides in midstream. He would no longer serve David, but would cast his lot with Absalom.[14] Absalom became the face of this revolution, but Ahithophel became the heart and soul. All along it would be Ahithophel who would drive the strategy, even to advising his new heir apparent to violate David's concubines. He would also be the one who would attempt to steer Absalom to attack David's encampment[15] and who promised to slay the king with his own hands.[16] In the meantime David had sabotaged Absalom's progress by sending in Hushai to counter the counsel of Ahithophel.[17] Absalom had cast his vote of confidence toward the counsel of Hushai, thus removing the favor of being his premier counselor.[18] This became a vote of confidence for Hushai and affected Ahithophel's standing in significant ways. "God had determined to discredit the counsel of Ahithophel so as to bring ruin on Absalom."[19]

Seeing that he had lost favor, Ahithophel withdrew from the company of Absalom. "When Ahithophel realized that his counsel was not followed, he saddled his donkey and left for his hometown. After making out his will and putting his house in order, he hanged himself and died. He was buried in the family tomb."[20]

Endnotes

1. syndein.com/ii_samuel_16.html -"Ahithophel was the Secretary of State. Normally, his advice was objective and respected by David, and by Absalom... It was the Absalom revolution, but it was Ahithophel who was the driving force behind it."

2. II Samuel 16:23 NLT - "Absalom followed Ahithophel's advice, just as David had done. For every word Ahithophel spoke seemed as wise as though it had come directly from the mouth of God."

3. II Samuel 16:23 MSG "The counsel that Ahithophel gave in those days was treated as if God himself had spoken. That was the reputation of Ahithophel's counsel to David; it was the same with Absalom."

4. II Samuel 11:14-15 MSG - In the morning David wrote a letter to Joab and sent it with Uriah. In the letter he wrote, "Put Uriah in the front lines where the fighting is the fiercest. Then pull back and leave him exposed so that he's sure to be killed."

5. II Samuel 11:3 notes that Eliam is the father of Bathsheba.

6. II Samuel 12:1-14 - Story of Nathan's visit to David, to bring him into accountability.

7. II Samuel 12:1-7 MSG

8. II Samuel 12:4 - There is a "traveler" in this story. Who is this traveler?

9. Maxie Thomas and I were good friends. We enjoyed his "One point sermons." That was his style of preaching. He is with the Lord, but I think of him occasionally. One of his best messages was about David's sin with Bathsheba and was entitled, "The Traveler."

10. The Treasury of David, by Charles H. Spurgeon - Psalm 55 - "It reads like a song of the time of Absalom and Ahithophel."

11. "Second Chances," by Max Lucado - Page 175 - Published by Thomas Nelson - ISBN 13:978-0-8499-4855-8

12. II Samuel 11:3 notes that Eliam is the father of Bathsheba.

13. Romans 12:18-21 MSG - "Don't hit back; discover beauty in everyone. If you've got it in you, get along with everybody. Don't insist on getting even; that's not for you to do. 'I'll do the judging,' says God. 'I'll take care of it.' Our Scriptures tell us that if you see your enemy hungry, go buy that person lunch, or if he's thirsty, get him a drink. Your generosity will surprise him with goodness. Don't let evil get the best of you; get the best of evil by doing good."

14. II Samuel 15:12

15. II Samuel 17:1-4

16. II Samuel 17:1-4

17. II Samuel 15:34

18. II Samuel 17:14

19. II Samuel 17:14

20. II Samuel 17:23 MSG

Chapter 28

THE BARZILLAI STORY

THIS GRANDFATHER WAS REMEMBERED LONG AFTER HIS PASSING

Barzillai was a grandfather that understood his current chapter of life and knew how he could best serve during this chapter. He had friends in high places, in unlikely camps, from years of living by solid principles and he drew on the currency with these friends to help King David in his time of need. Barzillai's heart was also to bless the next generation rather than himself. He truly wanted to turn "the hearts of the fathers to the children, and the hearts of the children to their fathers."[1] I would like to go into some detail to tell you his story, but first I must tell you the surrounding story about King David because these stories are intertwined.

The story of this grandfather is one, which shows us just how significant a role a grandfather can play. The battle was in full array, between the forces of Prince Absalom, and King David. So much had happened since Absalom had come to public view just four years[2] earlier, when he positioned himself at the gate of the city of Jerusalem. Allegiances had changed and loyalties had moved from the King, to his princely son. Absalom's coup d'état was in full attack mode and the lives of the King himself and all those who remained loyal to him were in jeopardy. It was clear that Absalom would spare no one who was loyal to his father.[3]

King David had called in his advisors and finally decided that the only option for him was to exit Jerusalem and the throne and allow God to fight his battles. So David and his servants left Jerusalem. Certainly Israel's army, led by Joab, was at their post, but David had left the final verdict in the hands of God. He hoped Absalom would be spared, but was not realistically facing the facts that, he who lives by the sword may also die by the sword.[4] The friends of David, the family of this king and all those who had commitments rallied and exited from Jerusalem. The mood among those occupying any public position was clearly that, you must cast your vote by walking, or you were casting your vote with the traitor. Everyone above the common folks of the land made quality decisions to exit with David, or be seen as loyal to the usurper. Those rallying behind and walking with David were his supporters.

BETTER IF ALL YOUR FRIENDS DO NOT RUN FOR COVER ... LORD GIVE ME FRIENDS TO BRIGHTEN MY DAY!

"David's humiliating flight from Jerusalem provoked two very different responses. Some heroically pledged themselves to serve David unto the death. Others took advantage of the situation to further their own interests or vent their anger toward the king."[5] While all of this was happening, Ittai stood with David to support him militarily; Zadok and Abiathar, joined in support of David, as priests of the Lord; the sage, Hushai, went to Jerusalem to be a double agent, favoring David, and working against the success of Absalom; Ziba, the servant from the house of Saul, proved that he was an opportunist, by betraying Mephibosheth; and finally, Shemei, cursed David.

David took a long and very painful personal inventory as he was leaving Jerusalem. Was he still the man whom God would choose again to be Israel's king? Yes, all those years ago God had clearly picked him out in the line up of brothers. But, David realized that he had failed God, he had failed himself, he'd failed his family, and now he had a son trying to bring it all down on his head.

As David looked to the embankment, to the side of the road, Shemei was cursing him. He asked himself, "Is it possible that God, if he could roll back time, would not choose me to be King?"

He'd heard the words of Nathan and they echoed deeply within his conscience and his very soul. All of these things had brought his third born son, Absalom into this conflict. David's response to the plea of Abishai to deal with Shemei now, finally came from the lips of the King, "No, Abishai, leave Shemei alone. Stand back and let God judge me and do with me as He wishes. I yield and I'm satisfied that God will let us know who is right and who should be king."

David heard the loyal remarks of those near him but decided that he would not harm Shemei, at this time, but would defer to God, allowing divine help in these matters. He determined that he would allow Shemei to continue his ranting, because, "perhaps God will see the trouble I'm in today and exchange the curses for something good."[6]

As the rebellion continued in Jerusalem, David depended on the counsel of Hushai and those who were loyal to him to give sound advice. Hushai sent word to David, by Zadok's two sons, Jonathan and Ahimaaz, runners in Israel's corps of runners who would take messages during times when communications were vital. The message to David advised him to cross over the Jordan before night came, because, otherwise calamity would come to him and all those with him. So, in the cover of darkness, David found refuge on the east side of the Jordan River.

The facts were that God would help David in spite of the mistakes he had made, because of his penitent heart, and would vindicate him with victory. Absalom was charging down a dangerous path, and those with him were in violation of significant principles. They would be defeated, but at the moment, chaos prevailed.

It was at this time that God brought into David's life a man of character and high principles. As David arose from his night of rest in Mahanaim, on the east side of Jordan, he saw, on the horizon three men coming bearing gifts. They came with donkeys, with servants, and with supplies to encourage, refresh, and revitalize this mass of people. They were friends from afar, when few of these pilgrims even suspected they had a friend; and they came in triplicate. Men of the Eastern Plateau, men of the highlands, reputed for their wisdom and kindness. Tough, but benevolent, strong but loyal, being generous to a fault. These were the kind of friends God had sent, and at a time when friends are better than gold.

These three men were Shobi, an Ammonite,[7] Machir from Lo-debar,[8] and Barzillai, the Gileadite.[9] These wealthy and generous men brought beds and blankets, bowls and jugs filled with wheat, barley, flour, roasted grain, beans and lentils, honey, and curds and cheese from the flocks and herds. They presented all this to David and his army to eat, "because," they said, "the army must be starved and exhausted and thirsty out in this wilderness."[10] Helping David was taking a risk. It was unlikely that Absalom would leave unpunished anyone who supported the rightful king. In showing loyalty to David, these men were being courageous.

David had dropped down into the backyard of loyal supporters. This region was not on the normal route to receive trendy communications. They were almost "an outpost," or a remote part of the land. The citizens who lived here were descendants of "Gad, Reuben and the half tribe of Manasseh," from the days when Joshua was leading all of Israel to cross Jordan. This lot had cast their desire toward the eastern plateau and wanted to stake their claim here in the east. Joshua had required of them to continue with the other tribes to cross Jordan and conquer Canaan, and so they had. Then they had faithfully come back across the Jordan to conquer their own land and settle there as tribesmen. The years had passed and they had created a remote culture slightly different to the rest of Israel. This was home to David, like he had not realized before. He was now among friends and the main conspirator[11] of the rebellion would not find them loyal to his usurping claims. The area where these men lived is what is now known as the Golan Heights[12] and is mountainous. The weather is different to the rest of Israel and nights are generally chilly all year long.

Barzillai was known as a Gileadite, and from the region, which produced the famed "Balm of Gilead." This balm, a medicinal salve, was the best healing ointment known in those times. It could be deducted that Barzillai had this balm in his heart, and was a healer of relationships. The conclusion drawn from reading this story is that Barzillai had been healing hearts his entire

> BARZILLAI HAD SOWN SEEDS OF FORGIVENESS AND PEACE YEAR AFTER YEAR, NOW GOD WAS SMILING ON HIM.

life. He saw that the land was in a civil war and that David was making his way to his part of the nation, as he fled from the threat of his own son, Absalom. This older man of peace, Barzillai, had sown seeds of forgiveness and calm to such a degree that he had formed an alliance between one, who had historically been loyal only to Saul, namely Machir, and another who was of the royal family of the neighboring nation of the Ammonites and enemies of Israel. When these three particular men had descended down the mountain terrain to meet this escaping king of Jerusalem and of Israel, it was quite a site to behold, because these men brought a currency of friendship that few could resist.

This story had begun long before we read of the man Barzillai. Barzillai had been a man with healing in his nature before he met with Shobi and Machir the first time. He listened to their complaints and nurtured them into a different world-view long before Absalom's betrayal. To look at them was to conclude that they were an eclectic team. Barzillai successfully forged them into a team of musketeers,[13] who were willing to take a chance to believe in a king who was God's man, but who had been humiliated by a prodigal son. Both Shobi and Machir had ample reason to resent David, but both had changed their minds, becoming convinced that David was the King to believe in.

Barzillai, being a very wealthy man, provided for the King and his family throughout the entire time David was in Mahanaim.[14] David was temporarily residing in Mahanaim, and Barzillai was living a distance away in another city called, Rogelim. Finally the battle was won and the "troops were beaten back by David's men. There was a great slaughter that day, and 20,000 men laid down their lives." Although Absalom tried to escape, he soon met his death at the hands of Joab.[15]

When the war was over, and Absalom was dead, Barzillai came down from Rogelim and accompanied the king to the Jordan River.

This man had enjoyed the visit of his king and David had enjoyed the hospitality of the highland people.

Now these two friends, David and Barzillai embraced on the east of Jordan never to see each other again. The Jordan River certainly would provide a geographical barrier and time, considering their ages would keep such a meeting from reoccurring. David was happy the war was finished, but could see that he had made a friend and was missing Barzillai's fellowship already. He ventured a question to Barzillai, by saying, "Cross the river and go to Jerusalem with me. I will take care of you." Barzillai declined the offer: "Your Majesty, why should I go to Jerusalem? I don't have much longer to live. I'm already eighty years old, and my body is almost numb. I can't taste my food or hear the sound of singing, and I would be nothing but a burden. I'll cross the river with you, but I'll only go a little way on the other side. You don't have to be so kind to me. Just let me return to my hometown, where I can someday be buried near my father and mother."[16]

It is not likely that the king only wanted to return the favor, by giving to Barzillai generosity and the necessities of life, as he was already a great man of wealth. Rather, it seems that David saw his own need of solid and wise counsel, to be available and nearby. To have a wise friend is always an advantage. Ahithophel, his former counselor, had betrayed him and was no longer alive.

If Barzillai would serve in the royal court, with a permanent place among his advisers, that surely would have been an honor, but he did not even consider the benefits of national acclaim or prestige. These had long ago fallen off of his list

> I DON'T HAVE ANOTHER RACE IN ME, BUT MY SON IS A THOROUGHBRED, AND HE WILL DO WELL, IF YOU TAKE HIM WITH YOU.

of appetites. Modesty and gentleness were more on Barzillai's list of desires.

Barzillai, being a true grandfather, as well as both wise and kind, took the occasion and said to his king, "Would you give your blessings to your servant Chimham,[17] just as you have wished to give to me? Would you let him cross over with my lord the king, and do for him whatever pleases you?"

David responded, also in the moment of parting friends saying, "Chimham shall cross over with me, and I will do for him what seems good to you. Now whatever you request of me, I will do for you."[18] Then all the people went over the Jordan. And when the king had crossed over, the king kissed Barzillai and blessed him, and he returned to his own place."[19]

Chimham is thought, generally to be the youngest son of Barzillai, and the one with the most future ahead of him. This was a break that a young man would appreciate very much. Historians believe that David made arrangements for Chimham to receive a grant of land from his own inheritance at Bethlehem. It seems quite apparent that David bestowed on him a possession at Bethlehem, on which, in later times, an inn or khan was standing.[20] It would retain Chimham's name for at least four centuries and is mentioned in Jeremiah as Geruth Chimham.[21] Some scholars have gone so far as to suggest that this was the location of the Inn, in Bethlehem, whose stable was used for the birth of Jesus Christ. If so, this is an amazing legacy for Barzillai and David, given that Jesus was called, the Son of David.[22]

SOME OF DAVID'S LAST WORDS WERE: "BE KIND TO THE SONS OF BARZILLAI, FOR HE WAS KIND TO ME IN DIFFICULT TIMES."

Finally, while laying on his deathbed, David gave instructions to Solomon, who was assuming the throne,

"Be kind to the sons of Barzillai of Gilead. Make them permanent guests at your table, for they took care of me when I fled from your brother Absalom."[23]

AN ADDENDEM

Who Were These Men, Really?
Note: Everyone has a History

These three men were Shobi son of Nahash, from Rabbah of the Ammonites, Machir from Lo-debar[24], and Barzillai, the Gileadite from Rogelim.

Shobi, Son of Nahash, the Ammonite King

Who was Shobi son of Nahash, from Rabbah of the Ammonites and what was his history with David the King? Also, why respond to David now, as he was actually an Ammonite?

* It was Shobi's father, Nahash, king of the Ammonites, who had humiliated most of the men of Jabesh, in the region of Gilead, by gouging out their right eyes, during the days of Saul, giving Saul the challenge that confirmed his being king of Israel.[25]

* When Nahash died, and his son, Hanun succeeded him, he proved to be very foolish. David decided to honor Hanun's father by sending delegates to give honor to Hanun, because of the kindness he had shown David in the past, during the days of Saul. It is likely that Nahash chose that he would be a friend with David, and therefore that made him less a

friend of Saul. It seemed expedient for David to remember his favorable response during those times.

* Hanun was the new, but young king, and had humiliated David's men by cutting off half of their beards and half of their robes, up to their buttocks, then sending them home in disgrace.[26]

* Notice that Rabbah, the hometown of Shobi was featured in the decisive battle against Nahash, and led by Joab.[27]

* Shobi's father was Nahash, and Shobi's brother was Hanun

Shobi's family had been close to Israel historically, and this Ammonite, son of Nahash, decided he would make things right by being kind to the man who really had never done his nation wrong. He saw things differently than did his Royal family.

Now, this alien, Shobi made a decision that he would not walk the path of his toxic family, but would respond with honor to the man he had respected from a distance. Surely the stories had been told over and again of his family's defeat, but now the truth had trickled down and eventually he could see that David had never meant anything but good to his brother, Hanun. His brother had listened to bad counsel and lost the day of favor that David had wanted to give to him. Now Shobi would do the right and the generous thing by accompanying Barzillai and take gifts of hospitality to David and his companions.

Machir from Lo-debar, Longstanding Friend of King Saul's Family

Who was Machir and what was his history with David the King? Saul's kingdom had come to a close upon his death and the death of his son, Prince Jonathan. The news of his death in the battle on top of Mt. Gilboa[28] came as tragic news to all those of the household of Saul. Immediately, news went throughout the land and especially to the house of Jonathan. When news came of the deaths of both Saul and Jonathan, the maid, in fear, picked up the five years old Mephibosheth, "and fled. But as she hurried away, she dropped him and he became crippled."[29]

Far away, on the other side of the Jordan, there was a safe place for Mephibosheth to grow up, away from the threat of execution, because Saul's family was no longer in power. This fear had caused them to want to hide the boy, on concern that he would be considered a possible usurper of the throne from David.

Machir was the man who had taken in the young crippled Mephibosheth when Saul's kingdom had ended. He had needed a home, a refuge, and new parents. This man and his family had been so kind. At first, when Ziba and David's soldiers had come to transport him to David and his palace, they had been concerned, as they were suspicious that it would all end in a bad way. However, from a distance, they had watched as the grace and love of a benevolent king had showered favor and acceptance upon the young man in his twenties. Now, he had enjoyed his meals at the King's table for a number of years and was quite wealthy, having been given all of the personal wealth of his grandfather, King Saul.[30]

MACHIR LISTENED AND DECIDED, "SAUL IS DEAD, AND DAVID IS MY KING." REDEMPTION WAS COMPLETE IN MACHIR'S MIND.

Now, this man Machir had seized on the opportunity to show generosity to the man he had grown to respect and serve. Of course, he would accompany Barzillai and take gifts of hospitality to David and his companions.

Endnotes

1. Malachi 4:6 NKJV

2. II Samuel 15:7 MSG "After four years of this, Absalom spoke to the king, "Let me go to Hebron to pay a vow that I made to God. Your servant made a vow when I was living in Geshur in Aram saying, 'If God will bring me back to Jerusalem, I'll serve him with my life.'"

3. 2 Samuel 15:6, 13, 14

4. www.gotquestions.org/live-die-by-the-sword.html ~ Question: "What does it mean to live by the sword and die by the sword?" **Answer:** The saying "live by the sword, die by the sword" is an idiom that basically means, "what goes around comes around." More to the point, "if you use violent, forceful, or underhanded methods against other people, you can expect those same methods to be used against you." The proverb "live by the sword, die by the sword" has a biblical origin. It comes from a conversation between Jesus and His disciple Peter just before Jesus was arrested in the Garden of Gethsemane… He told Peter to put his sword away, for "all who draw the sword will die by the sword" (Matthew 26:52)."

5. *History of Israel*, by James E. Smith, Ph.D. ~ History of Israel, 1000 years of Biblical Adventure. Copyright 2012, ISBN 978-1-105-75923-9, Page 310

6. II Samuel 16:12 MSG David said to those around him who wanted to slay Shemei, Here are the facts, "My own son, my flesh and bone, is right now trying to kill me; compared to that this Benjaminite is small potatoes. Don't bother with him; let him curse; he's preaching God's word to me. And who knows, maybe God will see the trouble I'm in today and exchange the curses for something good."

7. II Samuel 17:27 ~ Shobi was the son of Nahash, the Ammonite king, and brother to Hanun, who succeeded his father to the Ammonite throne.

8. Machir, from Lo-debar ~ The man who had taken in Mephibosheth when Saul's kingdom had ended, and the young lad, Mephibosheth was crippled in both feet, as a result of being dropped by the maid. He had needed a home, a refuge, and new parents. This man, Machir, had always been kind and generous and he was a friend, by nature. II Samuel 9:5

9. II Samuel 17:27 ~ Barzillai led this group of men to assist David, as he entered their area.

10. II Samuel 17:28 MSG ~ These 3 men generously supplied the needs of their guests.

11. Absalom, the prince and son of David.

12. www.bbc.com ~ The Golan Heights is legally a territory of Syria, but remains in dispute after it was taken by Israel during the Six Day War of 1967.

13. www.sparknotes.com/lit/3musk/section15.rhtml - The Novel called, "The Three Musketeers" by Alexandre Dumas is a historical novel. The author organizes his story around some of the major characters and events of 17th century French history. Cardinal Richelieu, Anne of Austria, and other important characters that really lived and acted at least roughly the way they do in the novel. In fact, the historical basis of Dumas's story extends all the way to his initial idea for the novel-- even to the Musketeers and d'Artagnan themselves.

14. II Samuel 19:32 - Barzillai had generously supplied David's needs during the war.

15. II Samuel 18:7-15 NKJV - Absalom is slain in battle, by David's general, Joab.

16. II Samuel 19:33-37 MSG -Barzillai graciously declines King David's generous offer.

17. Some of the Bible versions use the name of Chimham, while others use the spelling of: Kimham. I have chosen to use Chimham, due to the choice made by KJV.

18. www.biblestudytools.com - "probably the youngest son of Barzillai the Gileadite'

19. II Samuel 19:37-39 NKJV - Chimham left Barzillai's side and traveled with the King.

20. Smith's Bible Dictionary - Jeremiah 41:17 - This land was the property given to Chimham and later called, "Geruth Chimham," during the days of Jeremiah. Geruth means "The lodging places of," or as some say, "an inn."

21. Jeremiah 41:17-18 CEV - Jeremiah and those with whom he was traveling stopped by Geruth Chimham. Geruth means, "The lodging places of."

22. www.biblesnippets.com/inn-bethlehem - "Here is possibly a valuable lesson in the somewhat tenuous link between Jesus' birthplace and the kindness of Barzillai. These are the only two passages in the Bible, which refer to Chimham. For certain views of how God caused Scripture to be recorded, clearly every word is significant and there is likely to be a connection implied. Also, it wouldn't be surprising for David to have honored his promise by giving Chimham a plot of land near his hometown. To be balanced, I have this one filed under 'wouldn't be surprised,' Whether or not David's kindness to Barzillai directly connected him to Christ is immaterial. In countless ways their lives were interwoven, separated only by time; and we too hope to be part of the rich tapestry of God's plan for mankind." By Horace J. Wolf

23. 1 Kings 2:7 NLT - David gave instructions to favor the sons of Barzillai after his death.

24. Machir, from Lo-debar - The man who had taken in Mephibosheth when Saul's kingdom had ended, and the young lad, Mephibosheth was crippled in both feet, as a result of being dropped by the maid. He had needed a home, a refuge, and new parents. This man, Machir, had always been kind and generous and he was a friend, by nature. II Samuel 9:5

25. I Samuel 11 - Read the entire chapter to get the entire story

26. II Samuel 10:4 ~ King Hanun of the Ammonites humiliated David's visiting delegates.

27. II Samuel 12:26 AMP Now Joab fought against Rabbah of the Ammonites and took the royal city.

28. I Samuel 31:5 ~ The death of King Saul in battle on top of Mt. Gilboa.

29. II Samuel 4:4 NLT ~ Mephibosheth was dropped by his nurse, injuring both his feet.

30. II Samuel 9:9 ~ David gave to Mephibosheth the inheritance left by Saul.

Chapter 29

CHAORDIC
LIFE IS A BLEND OF BOTH
CHAOS AND ORDER

To experience transition is to "change from one thing to the next, either in action or state of being—as in a job transition or as in the much more dramatic example of a caterpillar making a transition into a butterfly."[1]

It is easy to assume you know and understand where you have been, and then to think you are clear on where you are going. At the same time it is the unknown that rattles the mind, because of not really grasping what lies ahead. It is therefore difficult to be prepared for transition and change, when you face so many variables. Taking a mature look at what you see, and then wrapping your mind around the characteristics of chaos will help you qualify for the challenge.

The circumstances of life do not come to us in perfect order and predictability. The ingredients of our lives are a blend of both chaos and order. Many people would prefer maintaining a certain order about every aspect of how they live life. In their perfect world of order and predictability they would choose to accept only the ideal and balanced. When things come from out of a clear blue sky,[2] they become frustrated and ill at ease. Their thinking is that chaos has nothing to do with reality. And yet, when too much of their lives lack risk then they will become boring cynics, and lacking in creativity and adventure.

THE SURPRISES AND THE ODD THINGS ARE WHAT BIRTH THE SERENDIPITIES OF OUR LIVES.

However, the reality of life is that, nothing is right until it has a healthy dose of chaos and unpredictability added in, so that we are reminded that we have a Creator who knows more than we know and is looking out for us to make sure we don't get too self-assured and satisfied with the way things are for us. The objective is to grow and living real life means that new ingredients must constantly be stirred into the mix of the cake we are cooking.

Introducing a New Word[3]: CHAORDIC

I'd like to introduce a word, which has meant a lot to me over the last decade or so. That word is chaordic[4]. To define the term chaordic is to realize that it is a blend of both chaos and order. Both are equal in value, and both are necessary for a good outcome.

There Are a Number of Life Experiences, Disciplines and Crafts, which would Confirm the Value of Chaos.

It is a fact that all the most powerful human emotions come from chaos. Consider fear, anger, and especially love. The very personality of love is chaos itself. Think about it! Love makes no sense. It shakes you up and spins you around…"[5] "Real love is always chaotic. You lose control; you lose perspective. You lose the ability to protect yourself. The greater the love, the greater the chaos. It is a given and that is the secret."[6]

A leader must appreciate that, while some things, by nature bring order, there are other things, which are chaotic, but still bring value.

When transition approaches, you would be wise to prepare for the unknown. Not all unknown ingredients are to be feared and avoided. Some of them seem a lot like viewing the tapestry from the underside. While you are going through transition it appears a lot like chaos, yet after the work is done, it has beauty and clarity. It is normal to hope that you could engineer the outcome and this amazing beauty; but it may be a surprise, as you are forced to acknowledge that your Creator, the master designer of the universe, is actually in charge, to a large extent. Of course choices will be made, but still there is a God and He controls what you can't.

For example, some transitions are micromanaged out of a fear of failure, so as to establish a guarantee of success and insure against losing face. To put it clearly, pride has a lot to do with many transitions, while, a total dependence, seasoned with lots of prayer and good counsel may be the winning recipe. We all want to keep ourselves safe but we cannot protect ourselves from everything. You just cannot manage every crisis, but must embrace life, by also embracing chaos.[7]

A Good Chef Needs Passion

It has been said that, "Not every cook is a chef." A cook is one who prepares food so that others can eat and satisfy their hunger. A chef is much more than just a cook, because of passion. A chef is able to blend expertise, passion and risk to a fine level of flavor and staging, so as to excite the interest of those who sit down to eat. It is not just about satisfying hunger, but also about engaging a number of other senses to excite and bring joy to the taste buds with unexpected flavors and aromas. A chef might introduce his creation by inviting you to sit with him to savor and experience the euphoria of taste. He might even say, "Let the fireworks begin." He or she knows that you will not be truly satisfied until you have stepped off the ledge and given yourself to the air-current flavors and updrafts of spice and exquisite oils and juices. Any good chef would tell you that the ingredients of a new dish must eventually be enhanced by flavors outside of your past experience and what you'd say is your perfect scenario of tastes.

CHAOS IS - THE ONION, THE CURRY, THE NUTMEG, THE OREGANO, THE PEPPER OR THE SALT ... THEY GIVE ATTITUDE TO THE DISH.

Often some limit their own growth and define themselves by saying, "I don't do spices. I am a meat and potatoes man," or, "I don't go for lamb or fancy fish. I prefer beef and sometimes chicken." Somehow they feel empowered by only accepting the normal flavors they grew up with. They are unwilling to venture out and off the ledge; they are afraid of heights and depths; they do not wish to fling themselves off into the world of new flavors, spices and aromas. If it is not familiar then they rule it out and will not step over the line. In the words of Tevye in the 1971 movie, Fiddler on the Roof, they are almost overheard declaring, "If I try and bend that far, I'll break."[8]

The facts are that if you continue to grow you will have to change in some significant ways. Food choices involve simple changes, but if you really wish to grow, then you must learn to grow in all areas. Recently I was reading about two caterpillars, which were talking when a beautiful butterfly floated by. One caterpillar turned to the other and said, "You'll never get me up on one of those butterfly things."[9] The sad truth is some people would rather stay the same than risk enough change to improve who they are and what they are capable of doing. Mediocrity really is a state of mind, which is not easily overcome. Some will take on mediocrity in their lives and deal with it to slay, as it were the dragon. Others will feel satisfied and affirmed by their lack of growth, thus confirming their personal and social demise of influence.

"They Look Kind of Funny, but They Sure Taste Good."

While living in the Black Forest of Germany my wife and daughter made some cookies for their contribution to an open house for a friend. One of the local French residents came in for the event. She was overheard saying to one of her friends: "Try these cookies. They look kind of funny, but they sure taste good." Such is life. Sometimes things look a little funny, or mixed up, but after going through all that it brings, we find they are palatable and quite pleasing. God is your Executive Chef. He will always surprise you when He displays on your table the ingredients He plans to use in preparation of your new favorite dish. You would never approve, in advance, of the way He plans to blend the oils, creams, sauces, and spices. Yet, after He does his blend of cutting, stirring, dicing and all with a wise use of heat and seasoning, you may find yourself thinking thoughts of satisfaction, if not overjoyed approval.

We have lost touch with the value of chaos, and how it seasons our every day walk through life. We think of chaos as a bad thing, when, in reality it brings a pungent and zesty element to our memories.

> "CHAOS WAS THE LAW OF NATURE; ORDER WAS THE DREAM OF MEN."
> —HENRY ADAMS
> THE EDUCATION OF HENRY ADAMS

If you have control issues and wish to micromanage your transitions, then I would ask that you consider holding your control issues at arms length, while you keep one eye on the ordered elements of your transition, and the other eye on the approaching chaos. You will be ahead of the game if you learn to mix it up in the bowl of your new Chaordic experience. Develop a sincere appreciation of chaos. Sometimes it is actually healthy to view order and chaos with equal suspicion. If you learn this art form, then you will learn to feel more comfortable with risk and more uncomfortable with "déjà vu."

Endnotes

1. www.vocabulary.com/dictionary/transition - "A transition is a change from one thing to the next, either in action or state of being—as in a job transition or as in the much more dramatic example of a caterpillar making a transition into a butterfly."

2. idioms.TheFreedictionary.com - "Out of a clear blue sky," or some say, "out of the blue." These are idioms from both America and Australia.

3. en.wikipedia.org/wiki/Dee_Hock - Coined by Dee Ward Hock (born 1929) is the founder and former CEO of the Visa credit card association. On March 3, 1993 he gave it in a dinner speech using, for the first time the term "chaord" and chaordic, a portmanteau combining the words chaos and order.

4. en.wikipedia.org/wiki/Chaordic - Chaordic - "The mix of chaos and order is often described as a harmonious coexistence displaying characteristics of both, with neither chaotic nor ordered behavior dominating."

5. www.goodreads.com/quotes/tag/chaos - Kirsten Miller, ___The Eternal Ones___

6. www.goodreads.com/quotes/tag/chaos - Jonathan Carroll, ___White Apples___

7. www.goodreads.com/quotes/tag/chaos - Susan Elizabeth Phillips, **Breathing Room**. - She made the statement that: "I finally figured out that not every crisis can be managed. As much as we want to keep ourselves safe, we can't protect ourselves from everything. If we want to embrace life, we also have to embrace chaos."

8. ___Fiddler on the Roof___, - movie, released in 1971 - A lavishly produced and critically acclaimed screen adaptation of the international stage sensation tells the life-affirming story of Tevye (Topol), a poor milkman whose love, pride and faith help him face the oppression of turn-of-the century czarist Russia. Running time: 3h 21m - Adapted from: Tevye and His Daughters, Fiddler on the Roof

9. www.squarewheels.com/content/teaching.html

THE LAST WORD
THE CONCLUSION OF
THESE MATTERS

In this book, "Is there a Grandfather in the House?" I have tried to introduce the young and the old. Yes, of course, they likely know each other, after all they have grown up in the same church or even in the same neighborhood, but in reality, they may not have made each other's acquaintance.

Grandfathers often appear to function above and aloof from the very young, because they are on a life assignment, that has brought to them significance and value that the young neither grasp nor understand. The older have been battle weary and wisdom laden, whereas the younger appear immature, in the minds of the aged. Still, each brings value to humanity, especially in light of the fact that the older ones will fade from the "earth scene" and join the great cloud of witnesses, while the young will take the place of the aged by becoming themselves "the old ones."

Have you discovered your story?

The older ones among us have a story to tell, and hope for an opportunity to tell it, while the young have a story to discover, but are often unaware of just how their journey should begin.

MAY I HAVE THIS DANCE?

We are often a lot like those sitting on the sidelines at a county social dance. The men on one side are glaring at the beautiful young girls opposite them, while the girls, all decked out in their fancy jeans, or evening dress are hoping one of those young men will get up the courage and ask "may I have this dance?" All are hoping, all are willing, but most are too shy to take the first step.

How are we to bless and advance this generation? Most of us would agree that, it has lost so much of the wisdom and righteous character, which was needed to improve society. Instead we are stumbling along like the awkward young and the bungling old needing, so desperately, to make a connection. We each have something to give to the other, but no one knows how to break the tie.

Now is the time and you have the keys of the kingdom. Whether you are the young leader or the older grandfather, you must stand up, throw your shoulders back, and release a burst of courage in your chest and step across the floor. If you are the young, like Terry Brisbane looking across at his grandfather, Bert Brisbane, then you must do what Terry did and take the long walk across the floor and say, "Granddad, would you teach me what 'church' is all about?" If you will do what Terry did then you could grow one of the biggest churches in your city?

Do not be intimidated, or neglectful of the Timothy, which God has sent to you.[1] If you are the grandfather then you must look at

264

your son in the Gospel as a reflection of yourself. If he is your Timothy, you must not see him as a young buck who wants your job, and wants to replace you and carry the church into the future. If God has sent him your way, then wake up and seize the moment; you must stand up and take the long walk across that floor. Step right up to the young man and ask if he would like for you to show him the ropes and how to lead?

MANY ARE SO COMMITTED TO "NOT DANCING" THAT THEY PASS AWAY AND NEVER LEARNED THE BENEFITS OF DANCING ... IT REALLY IS A BLAST!

* Will you seize upon the opportunity to redefine who you are?[2]

* Will you forget about "double honor"? Believe me it will come to you, if you don't ask for it.[3]

* Will you forget about the accolades of winning, and realize that, not only those who make up the great cloud of witnesses, but even you, at times, are cheering the baton onwards and to the victory flag?[4]

* And please stop singing that song, like Henry Higgens and Colonel Pickering, "I did it! I did it! I really did it!" And then will you go ahead and give some of the honor to the Guttersnipe, who deserves it?[5]

If you will do the things listed above, then that young person will continue talking about you long after you are gone?[6]

Failing to acknowledge the significance of these things will cause you to miss the mark, fail your assignment and forfeit your place in this majestic relay race. It doesn't matter how enormous your success is, by earthly standards; the fact is that heaven does not judge earthly accomplishments by earthly scales. God is supreme and above all others. In heaven 2+2 does not mean the same. God's equations arrive at different answers. The God factor must be considered when doing your calculations.

The angel is standing high up on the rock near the entrance of heaven, raising his trumpet upward and waiting for the order to commence blowing on the mouthpiece, to announce that time shall be no more. Jesus had said, "I will build my church." He has surely built it, but one more chapter remains before the command will issue from the mouth of God for that angel to announce the "times of the gentiles" are over.

You hold the key to whether this generation will be empowered to do its job, fulfil its assignments and put the capstone on Jesus' crowning achievement for this current generation. This generation is not just yours. It belongs to every member of the family: the children, the parents, the grandparents and the great-grandparents. But, let's not stop there; it also belongs to the great cloud of witnesses. We are too self-centered and often think it is about our generation of warriors. That is because we only see into the three-dimensional world we have grown accustomed to; but remember that if we could only unlock our creative juices, we would discover that the depth and breath of God's reality would take us to at least ten dimensions.[7]

Moses wrote about a revelation God had given him involving "synergy." He discovered synergy before the 19th century discovered it as a word.[8] He stated that one man can win over 1,000 of his enemy, and that is a fact that history bares out. But it is an additional fact that, when two link their arms together and march toward the enemy, that same man who will join with another man connecting them with the "God Factor"; then those two men can actually rout out 10,000 enemy. That is called the "God Factor."

"The 'God Factor' is that extra factor in the equation, which defies even the laws of nature and makes the impossible possible. It means standing on God's promises. It means that faith in Him overrides all impossibilities. God is in the heavenly realm, but He works in the real world. He deals, not just in spiritual blessings and rewards, but also in tangible, black and white, dollars and cents material blessings and rewards as well. He's the God of heaven, and also the God of this present world.

THE GOD FACTOR CHANGES ALL THE RULES ... HEAVEN'S MATHEMATICS ARE BETTER THAN YOURS.

He transcends both, rules in both, lives in both, dominates both, creates in both, and has the power to pay in both currencies."⁹

The reason we must add the God Factor to this equation is because of the last part of the verse in Deuteronomy 32:30. It states, *"How should one chase a thousand, and two put ten thousand to flight, except their Rock had sold them, and the Lord had shut them up?"* (to be defeated). So, between the fact that the god their enemy had trusted in had forsaken them, and that God took away their power to gain victory, then they would have had a chance to win. Because of the God Factor they were defeated and God's people were victorious.

If Grandfathers everywhere will link arms with sons and grandsons, we will change the world and truly be able to lend a hand to help Jesus build His church.

THE END

Endnotes

1. PROLOGUE: Is There a Grandfather in the House?

2. Chapter 15: Now is the time to Re-Invent yourself.

3. Chapter 1: Giving Double Honor when it is due.

4. Chapter 2: The Race is about the baton, not the runners.

5. Chapter 3: A Lesson in Point

6. Chapter 4: This generation needs Spiritual Fathers.

7. Science.howstuffworks.com/science-vs-myth/everyday-myths/see-the-fourth-dimension - Article: Can our brains see the fourth dimension? By Molly Edmonds

8. En.wikipedia.org/wiki/Synergy - SYNERGY - "the interaction or cooperation of two or more organizations, substances, or other agents to produce a combined effect greater than the sum of their separate effects. The words 'synergy' and 'synergetic' have been used in the field of physiology since at least the middle of the 19th century."

9. www.slideshare.net/bewitched123/the-god-factor - the God Factor

55434889R00181

Made in the USA
Charleston, SC
26 April 2016